BEYOND LIFE'S MOMENTS

BEYOND LIFE'S MOMENTS

AN EMPOWERING OUTLOOK ON TRANSCENDING UNEXPECTED SETBACKS

NICOLE SPINDLER

N Spindler

NEW DEGREE PRESS

BEYOND LIFE'S MOMENTS

An Empowering Outlook on Transcending Unexpected Setbacks

ISBN 978-1-63676-614-0 *Paperback*

978-1-63676-284-5 *Kindle Ebook*

978-1-63676-285-2 *Ebook*

To my incredible family for their unconditional love and support: Mom, Dad, and Corey.

To my interviewees who graciously shared their stories that will unfold in these very pages.

To all those who have been and will remain a remarkable part of my life's journey, making each moment greater than the last: grandparents, aunts, uncles, cousins, friends, neighbors, sorority sisters, professors, acquaintances, and coworkers.

This book is for you.

Thank you for being a part of my beyond.

CONTENTS

INTRODUCTION 11

PART 1. BRINGING LIFE'S CHALLENGING CHAPTERS TO LIGHT 19

CHAPTER 1. MY LIFE'S SUDDEN PLOT TWIST 21

CHAPTER 2. WHEN LIGHT BROKE THROUGH 31

CHAPTER 3. HOW DID WE GET HERE? 41

CHAPTER 4. EMPOWERING INSIGHTS 53

PART 2. THE EIGHT BUILDING BLOCKS 65

CHAPTER 5. GAINING PERSPECTIVE 67

CHAPTER 6. VULNERABILITY AND TRANSPARENCY 79

CHAPTER 7. RESILIENCY 91

CHAPTER 8. COMPASSION 103

CHAPTER 9. ADAPTABILITY 115

CHAPTER 10. GRATITUDE 125

CHAPTER 11. AUTHENTICITY 137

CHAPTER 12. SELF-CARE 147

PART 3. CONTINUOUS GROWTH AND THE LIVING PROOF 157

CHAPTER 13. JUST KEEP GROWING, GROWING, GROWING 159

CHAPTER 14. THREE TRANSFORMATIONAL TESTIMONIES 169

CHAPTER 15. REWRITING OUR PROFESSIONAL NARRATIVES 185

PART 4. OUT OF THE DARKNESS AND INTO THE BEYOND 201
CHAPTER 16. NEW BEGINNINGS, BARRIERS, AND BRIDGES 203
CHAPTER 17. FROM NOWHERE TO EVERYWHERE 213
CHAPTER 18. A REFLECTION 223

AFTERWORD 229
ACKNOWLEDGMENTS 233
APPENDIX 237

"Have a seat, sweet pea," said my mom as she pointed to the foot stool in the sunroom across from the teal sofa where my parents were sitting. I dragged the stool over to face my parents. A small mahogany coffee table displaying a noticeable number of pamphlets separated us.

"We wanted to discuss something with you," my mom calmly stated. I immediately straightened my posture to provide my undivided attention, placing my hands on my lap. My parents instantly turned to look at one another, grasping each other's hands tightly. My mom took several deep breaths before starting the conversation back up.

"Your father had several appointments with a variety of doctors this past week because, if you recall, he has been feeling intense pain and discomfort near his nose since the holidays."

I kept my gaze on my parents; my mom struggled to process her thoughts into words, and my father avoided eye contact with me completely, keeping his head bowed. He was silent and seemed to be hiding something from me. I attempted to display poise and composure, but inside I was shaking with fear. Stress was building up in my stomach all the way through the back of my throat.

My mom spoke and nearly choked on her words. "They found something . . . unexpected . . . ." She turned away for a moment, attempting to regain enough strength to finish her sentence as a tear trickled down her cheek.

My body shook while my heart pounded uncontrollably in my chest. It felt like my breaths were cut short every single time I inhaled. My mom's next words pierced my heart and soul; it would be that next sentence on January 13, 2012—my dad's birthday—that forever redefined my life as I knew it:

"Nicole, your father has cancer."

INTRODUCTION

BETTER BECAUSE OF IT

It is remarkable how four words, one sentence—a single moment—completely turned my entire world upside down and inside out. Yet, what emerged during this derailment in my family's life was nothing but light, love, and life. In fact, this quote from Kim Chambers perfectly captures how I perceived my dad's battle with cancer and other setbacks that I have encountered during my life's journey:

"Who would have thought that my injury was the best thing that ever happened to me? If this never happened to me, I would never be where I am today. I felt like I was given this gift that I had to work through, to push the boundaries of what is possible, and to find my best self on the other side."

This perspective, which I admire and embody, is how Chambers describes her transformational journey to become one of the world's top marathon open-water swimmers. In 2007, thirty-year-old Chambers was rushing to work when she tripped and fell down a staircase; she woke up in a hospital hours later, realizing the surgeons had saved her right leg from amputation with barely thirty minutes to spare.

During the accident, Chambers experienced blunt force trauma to her right leg and was later diagnosed with Acute Compartment Syndrome (ACS). This exceedingly rare condition occurs when the tissue pressure within a muscle builds up from internal bleeding, resulting in persistent tightness and tissue swelling, bruising, numbness, and intense, sharp pain. ACS not only requires emergency surgery but also has a dire prognosis of a less than 1 percent chance of walking unassisted.[1]

After two years of extensive physical therapy, Chambers was still severely disabled; she had massive scars on her leg, walked with a limp, and required a specially made orthotic for her right foot. Despite these setbacks, she craved the freedom to move again and decided to try swimming. Once Chambers was in the water, she found that she no longer felt disabled—she felt limitless and free.[2]

Throughout the next chapter of Chambers' life, her perseverance flourished; in November 2009—only a few months after first attempting to swim—Chambers decided to brave the chilly waters of the San Francisco Bay, which sparked her passion for swimming.

From 2012 to 2014, Chambers became one of only seven people to complete the Oceans Seven challenge, and in August

1 "Story: At the Podium," Kim Swims, accessed October 2, 2020.

2 Ibid.

2015, she became the first woman to swim from the Farallon Islands to the Golden Gate Bridge, a route covering approximately thirty miles.[3]

Chambers could have let her diagnosis define the rest of her life, surrendering to debilitating thoughts of fear, self-doubt, and uncertainty that became her new reality. Yet, she turned her condition into an uplifting opportunity that reaped numerous personal and professional achievements.

* * *

One way or another, we all will be faced with at least one of life's greatest challenges. These challenges can inflict physical, emotional, spiritual, and mental harm on us and our loved ones, leaving us in an unsettling state of shock and denial. Common examples of distressing events include major surgery or life-threatening conditions, mental illness, divorce, moving to a new location, physical pain or injury, natural disasters, abuse, harassment, unexpected deaths of loved ones, shootings, pandemics, war, and imprisonment.

When faced with a traumatic event, people have difficulty understanding why they were the victim. Continually struggling with persevering through uncertainty and setbacks can have detrimental effects that can impede one's aspirations and compromise their well-being. According to the American Psychological Association, not being able to overcome life's unexpected obstacles can have long-term manifestations,

---

3 *Stories,* "How Kim Chambers Conquered the 7 Deadliest Swims," May 28, 2015, video, 4:47.

including the development of post-traumatic stress disorder (PTSD) and other anxiety disorders, substance abuse or addiction, depression, isolation, insomnia, extreme emotional outbursts or mood swings, somatic symptoms, cardiovascular disorders, intense fear of future events or recurrences, and worsening or development of a medical condition.[4]

Not succumbing to negative reactions when faced with an unexpected life event can be very difficult. Some people feel it is easiest to accept they're a victim and give in to despair. If someone with a victim mentality experiences uncertain stressors or obstacles like a medical diagnosis, they would perceive most aspects of their life to be negative and out of their control; they would fear they have little power to change things or make improvements because they would believe these challenges were directly targeted at them.

I believe an unexpected derailment in life can be conceptualized as a revolving door of infinite possibilities that can have positive implications—not just in your defining moment, but throughout your life's journey.

* * *

My optimistic outlook on distressing challenges emerged from my own personal experience. At age fifteen, my dad's cancer diagnosis made my heart stop beating, shook me to the core, and redefined my life and existence. I became unwillingly immersed in a life-altering event that was

4 Soo Jeong Youn and Raquel Halfond, "How to Cope with Traumatic Stress," *American Psychological Association,* October 30, 2019.

unfolding right in front of me, not only as a witness but also as a central protagonist in the story, I had firsthand experience with the impacts and consequences that this distressing event had on me and my family.

Upon hearing the unexpected news, I made a pivotal decision that redefined my unexpected derailment: I chose to be optimistic and to see where this journey would take me and my family in the years to come. I refused to fall endlessly through the rabbit hole of negativity that would drown me in sorrow, denial, and self-pity.

Little did I know, opting for positivity when undergoing challenges would serve me extraordinarily well. The lessons I learned during my obstacles not only allowed me to prevail through the initial crisis, but also succeed through my collegiate years and in my Human Resources and Management career.

> I believe that my initial life-altering obstacles were one of the greatest things that have ever happened to me, and I would not change anything about it.

Over the years, I have had the greatest privilege of both witnessing and learning from experts such as my friends, fellow students, acquaintances, and colleagues. Whether dealing with life-threatening illnesses or struggling with mental health and anxiety, the people I know in this book have overcome obstacles and experienced triumphs. They're all exceptionally grateful that their obstacles sparked their transformation into the people they are today. They continually inspire me.

Hearing so many stories of hardships led me to an idea: I should write a book that verbalizes, showcases, and illustrates living proof that we all have opportunities to continuously grow through and beyond our obstacles. I hope this book can provide some guidance or comfort to those who have or are currently struggling to overcome a major life challenge. This book will also speak to people who are going through a change or transition in their life and are looking for a different way of perceiving and cherishing all the moments that make up their life's journey.

Times of change and uncertainty are critical thresholds in our lives that provide an infinite number of moments waiting to be seized and enjoyed. These moments can also demonstrate opportunities to adopt and reinforce the lessons within the pages of this book.

* * *

Throughout this book, I will bring to light my first and most meaningful hurdle in my life—my father's extraordinarily rare cancer—while illustrating how the lessons I learned during my initial derailment positively and directly leveraged my collegiate years and professional passions.

I will also share eight guiding principles that withstand the tests of trauma and time. These principles reveal themselves during our life's challenges and work cohesively to drive you toward the biggest objective for overcoming obstacles: continuous growth. Finally, this book will demonstrate how the lessons and principles acquired through distressing events can have direct implications in the professional settings and can positively transform employees, leaders, and managers.

Let's take this next step forward by turning the page. I will lead you on a journey of self-growth and help you discover all the wonderful things that await you in the midst of and beyond your life's moments. The beyond is already waiting for you at the end of the tunnel.

during our 1:1 sessions and work cohesively to drive you toward the biggest objectives [illegible] time [illegible] word. [illegible] [illegible] [illegible] [illegible] through [illegible] [illegible] [illegible] [illegible] [illegible] [illegible] [illegible] [illegible]

[illegible] next step forward in [illegible] [illegible] [illegible] [illegible] of self [illegible] [illegible] wonderful [illegible] toward [illegible] [illegible] and your best [illegible] [illegible] the end of [illegible]

PART I

BRINGING LIFE'S CHALLENGING CHAPTERS TO LIGHT

CHAPTER 1

MY LIFE'S SUDDEN PLOT TWIST

PITTSBURGH, 2012

Two weeks prior to my father's birthday, he had trouble breathing through one of his nostrils. One of the three medical professionals my dad visited originally hypothesized it to be a polyp, but a specialist noticed something unexpected in my dad's nose after revisiting one of his computed tomography (CT) scans. A day later, my dad went to a neurologist to take a closer look at his examination and to do a magnetic resonance imaging (MRI). The tests ultimately unveiled that a tumor had formed in the bridge of his nose close to the brain's frontal lobe, specifically in the olfactory nerve that transmits impulses from the nose to the brain.

My dad's diagnosis was olfactory neuroblastoma, a very rare cancer and a type of nervous system disease accounting for roughly 5 percent of all cancers of the nasal cavity and paranasal sinuses and 2 percent of all sinonasal tumors. It develops in the cribriform plate, the bone deep within the skull between the eyes and bridge of the nose, and in the nerve tissue associated with the sense of smell called the olfactory nerve. No one understands the cause of olfactory neuroblastoma; doctors cannot even confirm whether or not environmental or genetic factors are involved in the development of this cancer.[5]

In January 2012, a doctor in the otorhinolaryngology field, Dr. Snyderman—who happened to be, of all places, at the University of Pittsburgh Medical Center (UPMC) Presbyterian hospital located in my hometown of Pittsburgh, Pennsylvania—was pioneering the research and treatment for olfactory neuroblastoma. Fewer than a dozen people were known to have been diagnosed with this cancer before my dad. Most of them did not survive beyond a couple of years, leaving my family on an unprecedented journey with an unknown survival rate looming over our heads.

"We're incredibly fortunate that the doctors discovered this when they did," my mom stated, catching tears as she explained to me what had befallen my dad. "They said that if they never found it . . . if they didn't suspect that there was something off during the examinations, your dad might not have lived beyond a year."

I was in utter disbelief and unable to comprehend the unthinkable. My mind was inundated with questions as I

5 "Olfactory Neuroblastoma (Esthesioneuroblastoma)," UPMC: Life Changing Medicine; "Olfactory Neuroblastoma," John Hopkins Medicine.

gazed at the table scattered with an array of pamphlets, test results, and medical forms.

Our family became consumed by the unknowns, uncertainties, and firsts: how this cancer could have developed, how the surgery scheduled for February 10, 2012 would be one of the first of its kind, and how the post-surgery recovery would evolve every day with the long-term effects being mere guesses . . . assumptions . . . hypotheses . . ..

How could this happen to my dad—the healthiest and most active person I knew—who ran five miles every day? What if my dad never celebrates another birthday, doesn't get to witness me graduating high school and going off to college, or can never walk me down the aisle when I get married?

Never did it cross my mind, until that day, that my dad's life could end so suddenly and unexpectedly.

Sitting in the sunroom in the midst of a wintry afternoon in Pittsburgh, I soaked up every drop of information my parents shared. The room was a void of silence for quite some time, all three of us sitting there, listening to each other's breaths and sniffles.

Suddenly, my dad brought us all back to the present moment by asking, "Can you promise me something, sweetheart?"

I slowly turned toward him, using every muscle in my body to hold back the tears and give him my undivided attention.

"I want you to promise me that no matter how challenging it gets, no matter what happens, I want you to continue to focus on your academics and lacrosse. Most importantly, I want you to stay strong and determined to fight this with me."

Although everything surrounding our family's new circumstances was overwhelming, I made one of my most important decisions in that moment.

Without any hesitation or afterthought, I made *the* decision.

I chose to see this through until the very end.

I was passionately committed to fight this alongside my dad.

I wanted to see where this unexpected journey would lead us.

I aimed to walk confidently into the unknown with my head held high, embrace positivity, and see all the good lessons and opportunities that would manifest to us in the present and in the years to come.

As I looked intently into my dad's eyes and brushed the tears off of my blushed cheeks, I only had enough strength to say, "I promise, Dad; cross my heart."

* * *

Determined to keep my promise to my dad, I booked one of the first available appointments at my high school's counseling center. Within the safe, invisible force field of my guidance counselor's office, I entered an alternate reality, away from the drama that bubbled and boiled over in the halls of high school.

I divulged my intentions to my guidance counselor about continuing to achieving excellence and still being the passionate student, athlete, and friend who I always was; this conversation provided reassurance that my current circumstance wouldn't impede my ability to enjoy my academics, extracurricular activities, and overall life.

"I want my teachers to realize that despite my unfortunate circumstances, I'm still willing to put forth the time and effort into the coursework," I stressed to my guidance counselor. "I promised my father that I would make him proud."

Following my appointment and an email sent to all my teachers detailing my father's diagnosis, I worked tirelessly to muster up the courage to approach and share these uncertain times with my close friends, teachers, and lacrosse coaches. Additionally, I strove to uphold the promise that I made to my dad by putting even more effort into my coursework and lacrosse because I knew it wouldn't only ensure that I stay in a positive mental headspace, but it would also keep my dad's strength up and make him proud of me.

I became the only freshman who attended every single lacrosse drop-in (practices before try-outs) and attended regular one-on-one meetings with my teachers to assure I was striving for exceptional marks in each class. Prioritizing the importance of academics, activities, and sports kept me focused, maintained my positivity, and proved to be a great distraction when fear and anxiety started to creep in.

The long three weeks prior to the surgery were overflowing with immense support, encouragement, and prayers from family, close friends, and neighbors. We received everything from casseroles from my lacrosse coach and a fellow teammate to a card with inspirational messages and a bouquet of flowers from the neighbors. We also spent these three weeks trying to learn every morsel of information we could from the surgeon about my dad's ever-developing cancer. Even though every day felt like a climb up Mt. Everest, I still appreciated how fortunate I was to have amazing friends, coaches, and teachers. Their overwhelming support strengthened our relationships while continuously uplifting my family's determination to persevere through our current circumstances.

* * *

The inevitable—yet highly anticipated—surgery day finally arrived. We were on our way to the hospital by 4:30 a.m., accompanied by one of my aunts, who lived five minutes away. I held my dad's hand the entire way in the complete darkness of the journey, absorbing his stillness and tranquility. If it was possible, our hands probably would have produced a beam of light, shining brighter than the night skyline of Pittsburgh and illuminating the Fort Pitt Tunnel.

After we checked in at the hospital and signed the remaining waivers, a young man wearing a white doctor's coat with a clipboard tucked under his arm walked through the double doors of the lounge entrance.

"Mr. Spindler, are you ready?" he asked.

"We will be right with you," my father replied. My father stepped away from the front desk and bent his knees slightly toward the ground to be face-to-face with me. He took my hand and placed it in his, saying, "Stay strong, sweetheart. I promise that things will get better in the end."

He kissed me on my forehead, stood up tall with his head held high, his hand slipping away from my grasp as he turned to follow the doctor. My mother took his arm and walked alongside him through the lounge doors. They headed to the preoperative room where my dad would get one last rundown of his extensive surgery before being given anesthesia.

I stood planted where my father left me, not realizing he left my side and still feeling the warmth of his hand imprinted on mine. My aunt managed to successfully guide me toward the lounge area where we took our seats . . . and waited. With no estimated end time to this extensive, risky surgery, I silently prayed for the perseverance of the surgeons to save my dad and for my dad's determination to prevail during these challenging yet defining moments.

My mom returned to the waiting room an hour later. We received no official word of how things were going until the tracking monitor nearby flashed my dad's patient number on the screen.

At 7:02 a.m., next to my father's patient number flickered the words:

"Surgery Started."

* * *

The subsequent hours spent in the windowless waiting room consisted of dozing off occasionally, reading, going to the cafeteria, and staring off into the distance. Late in the morning my dad's mother and his sister arrived at the hospital and planned to spend a few days in Pittsburgh to support us. In the early afternoon hours, approaching two o'clock, a nurse frantically looked for my mom; apparently, the surgeon wanted to speak with her. As my mom rushed off to speak with the surgeon, internally I was screaming for the entire universe to hear:

"What happened to my dad?"

There was a *slight* complication . . .

The removal of the tumor would take exponentially longer than anticipated. While the surgeons worked to eliminate all the traces of the tumor, doctors examined the benign mass in their laboratory. Since such a tumor was an unfamiliar spectacle in medical practices at the time, this extensive examination was essential before they could proceed with stitching my dad back together.

At 7:45 p.m., after watching the Pittsburgh Penguins finish the first period of their game on the television in the empty waiting room, a message popped up on the monitor indicating my dad's surgery was completed. My mom sped over to the front desk and asked the nurses to escort her to see my dad in the recovery ward.

An hour later, my mom returned to the waiting room and told us that my dad was alright and was starting to come around after being under anesthesia for over twelve hours. All five of us walked to the room that my dad was recovering in. As I peered into the room, I saw my dad on a stretcher. Afraid of what he might look like post-surgery, I cautiously approached. My nerves subsided as I caught a glimpse of my dad; he looked pale and tired, with several tubes across his face and bandage-like packing wrapped around his head and parts of his face.

He could barely talk, but he did for me.

"Is that you, Nicole?" my dad spoke in a dry, scratchy low voice.

"Yes, it is. Hi, Dad," I paused as a waterfall of emotions and relief cascaded over me. "I love you," I said as I started to cry.

"I love you too," he said.

One of the doctors pushing the stretcher said, "Your father is a brave man. We were all pretty impressed with him. Ha-ha! We all thought he was thirty!"

I smiled at that thought and moved aside as the doctors and nurses got my dad settled into his room. Before leaving the hospital, I caught one last glimpse at the miracle that would be occupying that room for the next several days.

On the way home that night, I truly didn't know what to think or how to feel, especially after an exhausting sixteen hours. I was nervous about the success of my dad's surgery, afraid

I would not recognize him after the tumor was removed, and worried that this cancerous derailment might weaken my family dynamics. Yet in the car, I felt those initial fears wash away after the successful completion of the surgery and seeing my dad again. What replaced my fears was the powerful, definitive notion that perhaps both working through and overcoming my dad's diagnosis would only make our family stronger . . . our lives more meaningful.

I was certain that I felt the divine blessings of God, family, friends, neighbors, doctors, the community, and the city of Pittsburgh surrounding us. In that moment, I enjoyed the balance and stillness from the backseat, catching the last glimpse of the Pittsburgh skyline reflecting in the Monongahela River before vanishing into the Fort Pitt Tunnel.

CHAPTER 2

WHEN LIGHT BROKE THROUGH

I spent two monotonous, twelve-hour days visiting my dad at the hospital. Nurses worked effortlessly to make sure his IVs were hooked up, his heart rate was stable, and the packing inside his nose and around his head was fresh every hour. My mom ran to-and-fro to assist my dad in any means possible, and my grandmother and my dad's sister would rotate shifts in the guest lounge and in my dad's room. Meanwhile, I simply occupied a chair against one of the walls of my dad's hospital room; I refused to leave my seat out of fear that something would happen to my dad if I weren't around.

On Monday, I felt awful returning to school after being at my dad's side for the entire weekend. I tried to concentrate on the material being presented in my classes—especially after missing last Friday because of the surgery—but I could not stop thinking about my dad. I worried if he was able to keep down his medicine, get some rest, and make enough progress to be able to return home soon. I felt like if I stayed at the hospital long enough, something would come up for me to do to help my dad feel better. Yet, the promise that I made to him rang in my ears, reminding me that being at school was the best thing I could do to keep my strength up and make my dad proud.

The next day, on Tuesday, February 14, I returned home from school and climbed up my steep street after being dropped off at the bus stop. I punched in the code to unlock the garage door and headed into the basement. I was mentally preparing to immerse myself in my abundant load of homework. As I was untying my shoes, I heard my mom talking to someone. No other car except my family's was in the driveway when I arrived home and, as far as I was aware, we were not expecting any visitors today.

Then, I recognized a familiar voice.

I leaped upstairs and pushed the basement door wide open to reveal one of the most amazing sights: my mom and dad talking in the kitchen together. Everything inside of me melted like snow, warming my body, heart, and soul that had been stone cold for the last month. My parents looked in my direction. I stared right at my father, tears running down my cheeks. I managed to cry out, "DAD!"

* * *

Although my dad was discharged from the hospital earlier than anticipated, we were still only in the beginning stages of our family's extraordinary life journey. The stark alterations in my dad's appearance started with significant weight loss that I had not noticed before, but then I remembered it had been over a week since my dad had a proper meal. Additionally, there was the heavy packing in his nose and a row of staples across a sliver of his head—which the otolaryngologist surgeon had inserted—that had been concealed by the bandages at the hospital. The removal of the tumor also resulted in taking extensive time to patch up my dad's skin around his face.

My dad occupied himself by attending several appointments each week, sleeping in one of the chairs in the sunroom because the staples prevented him from lying flat on his back, and struggling to keep down any fluids or soft foods. He was unintentionally disengaged in most aspects of his previous life except for wanting to regain this strength so he could run again. I hardly ever saw him awake. My mom's full-time job became being my dad's caregiver, and I did everything in my power to stay strong for my dad.

No matter what, I always found something good to appreciate each day during his recovery, whether it was my dad being able to eat a little more than before or getting a good report from the doctor after one of his appointments. The small, yet gradual progress my dad made during these moments gave me more than enough determination to fight this alongside him.

During this uncertain time, my mom and I remained inseparable. Although she was scared and feared the unexpected, she did not falter once in her role as my mom. She became the glue of our family, working to keep a sense of normalcy as much as possible. Whether it was attending as many of my lacrosse games, banquets, and teacher meetings as she could or frequently checking in with my brother at school and guiding him during his switch in majors, she did everything to stay active in our lives and to keep our family moving forward.

With this new, life-altering situation overtaking our lives, my mom embodied relentless strength and a determined spirit. Even when she was consumed with her own challenges, day in and day out, she kept her strength for me. She prioritized our talks and check-ins where we would share how we were feeling and handling recent news. She also protected me from carrying all the burden that the cancer prognosis threw in our family's direction. She has been more than my mom; she is my role model, my best friend, and my rock.

Roughly two months after the surgery, my dad embarked on the next stage of his recovery: intense radiation every day for two full months. After each radiation treatment my dad was left tired and not feeling well. Gradually, he lost most of his hair and his weight dropped to barely 128 pounds. During the treatments, more unexpected news flooded into our lives: the radiation oncologist and neurologists confirmed that my dad would eventually lose his entire sense of smell and some of his ability to generate saliva, making it difficult to eat various foods or digest properly.

Miraculously, my dad's strength, relentlessness, and determination did not falter throughout all the strenuous yet crucial appointments, radiation treatments, and enduring discomfort. He placed his energy and focus on our family, his recovery, and the Word of God, knowing there was an abundance of gifts and positive moments forthcoming in our lives.

* * *

Lacrosse and my freshman year of high school came to a close in May, bringing not only blooming flowers but also my brother, Corey, who came home from college for the summer. This was the first time he saw our dad since the Christmas holiday.

While my parents and I were in Pittsburgh dealing with our new reality, Corey was a sophomore at Ohio State University in Columbus, Ohio. On several occasions, I envied my brother. I thought he was fortunate because he, unintentionally, dodged our troubles, didn't sit through a twelve-hour long surgery, maintained a social life, and didn't seem to experience the roller-coaster of emotions and thoughts that I had. I admit, I was partially closed-minded and naive because I thought he would never fully understand what I battled with on our family's home front.

One afternoon during summer vacation, my brother admitted to me how difficult it was for him to be over three hours away with no car, swamped with coursework, reevaluating his choice of major, and in a state of overwhelming sadness, shock, and helplessness. Initially, he didn't know how he could provide our family support from afar. My brother described his role in our family's circumstances as "not having a role." Like the promise I made to our dad, the only thing Corey thought he could do was simply power through each day and do well in his classes.

By chance, within the initial days of hearing about our dad's life-threatening condition, my brother became heavily involved with his Fraternity and BuckeyeThon, the Ohio State University's twenty-four-hour dance marathon that raises money for families with children diagnosed with pediatric cancer.

"I got to personally meet and work with families who were fighting their own battles too," my brother told me about his first time being a part of BuckeyeThon.

"I thought that it was a good avenue for me because I could give back, put my blood, sweat, and tears into an organization, since I couldn't do much for dad the last several months," Corey revealed.

By attending a large, diverse university and being a part of this remarkable opportunity to change the lives of a handful of families, my brother acquired an immense perspective that reassured me that our family was going to get through these uncertain times: "I realized that we aren't alone and cancer is a greater issue than anyone realizes, impacting all our lives in more ways than one. There is nothing about it to be ashamed of; it wasn't bad luck—it's common, and it's also common to get through these challenging times."

As my brother unveiled the truth about his personal hurdles during his spring semester, I sensed his helplessness and frustration that he was not at home. I was glad he found closure in supporting others who battled a comparable disease. He turned our dad's diagnosis into an optimistic catalyst to cherish life's precious moments. I was truly proud of my brother.

Through both Corey's involvement with BuckeyeThon and the opportunities I had to meet with and listen to several individuals' stories about their encounters with cancer through news and events, we discovered that scores of families have been and are currently being impacted by cancer. Some of these impacts can be positive; uncertain times can bring people together. Our family's uncertain setback brought my brother and I closer together, instilling the fact that we have more in common than we realized. Our sibling love flourished and strengthened after openly sharing our thoughts and emotions over the past several months with each other. Most importantly, although my brother and I were both fighting our own personal battles during our dad's enduring diagnosis and recovery, we both knew our family would emerge from this struggle victoriously.

* * *

The dragging, sweltering late spring and summer days didn't prevent my dad from making slight, yet steady progress. By the end of July when my dad completed all his radiation treatments, the skin on my dad's face and scalp were healed with some minor, faded scaring, and his hair gradually started to grow back. The lead doctor and medical specialists were astounded by the miraculous progress my dad had made, surpassing the predictions and uncertainties that were originally roadblocks on my dad's path. Preceding the praise and high hopes after my dad's endless strand of appointments, we got the "all-clear" from the lead doctor to schedule a procedure during the first week of August to remove the staples and packing in his nose.

After the procedure and throughout the rest of the summer, I caught glimpses of my dad in the sunroom. He would be reading the Bible, carefully turning each page, and setting intentions through the power of prayer. The reading lamp cast an aura around my dad like a halo and the wings of an angel. I remained still at a distance, admiring his improvements, and soaking in these moments. I enjoyed these times with my dad, even if they were silent.

I marveled at how remarkable my dad's recovery had been thus far. His hair was starting to grow back thick enough to cover up the scars from the staples, his skin was less dry, and his face and body were fuller and looked healthier. He made constant efforts each day to walk around our house or down our street a few houses at a time, gradually working to regain his strength so he could eventually run again.

I recognized, reflected, and appreciated how much good had already come from my dad's recovery, like fireworks lighting up a clear, summer night sky: the marvelous recovery my dad was making, the tightly knotted ties of my family and friendships, the overwhelming support from numerous compassionate individuals, and the excellence and excitement I discovered through my academics, activities, and interests. My dad still had quite a bit more climbing to do, and uncertainty still lingered in the shadows, but there was hope.

That is all we need.

That is all I needed.

* * *

The end of August brought the start of a new school term. It was the first day of my sophomore year of high school. I raced out the door and walked down my street's steep hill in strides at 6:45 a.m., a mixture of dew and sunlight draping the entire neighborhood. About a block away, I turned to find two other high school students waiting at the next stop sign; however, my gaze was fixated on something else that morning.

I saw a figure running toward the bus stop, the details becoming clearer with every step: it was a man, about fifty years old, wearing a black and green quarter-zip jacket, black shorts, and grey shoes. He was running at a steady pace. The haze made it difficult to see who it was. But wait . . . No way! I felt like a brick had hit me. I could not believe it: my dad was in front of me. And he was running. It was the first time he had run since the day before his surgery. He was alive, and there before me.

Unconsciously, I jumped up and down, shaking with pure joy and anticipation. I tried to get his attention. It was really him! The moment was surreal; I could hear the music from the "Run, Forrest, run" scene from *Forrest Gump* playing in my mind and ringing in my ears. As my dad ran toward me, I yelled for him to keep running, just like Jenny told Forrest.

Upon reaching my bus stop, I said, "Hi Dad! I love you!!"

Tears of joy ran down my face. My neighbors probably thought I was crazy. But I didn't care. That was my father; I was so proud of him and even prouder to be his daughter.

"I love you too," my dad called out, with no shortness of breath, as he ran past me and toward the neighborhood entrance.

Moments later, the bus arrived at our stop. Before boarding the bus, I turned my head to my left in the direction where my father was heading. He was clearly visible, running toward our neighborhood. I was overwhelmed with abundant happiness.

I took the biggest sigh of relief as I found my seat at the back of the bus, catching one more glimpse of my father.

Seeing my dad running that morning was one of the greatest and proudest moments of my life. It was the ideal start to perhaps some of my greatest years of my life.

I couldn't believe that the positive intentions I instilled back in January held true to this moment. The fact that my family and I championed through our life-altering obstacle was living proof that light, optimism, and good will radiate even in the most adverse times.

As the bus drove around a bend, I saw my father run toward the rising sun in the distance. Toward the start of the new day and the journey ahead . . .

Toward the light at the end of the tunnel.

CHAPTER 3

HOW DID WE GET HERE?

You are traveling along ceaseless, windy, worn-down roads that bend at irregular intervals and cascade down deep valleys after summiting steep inclines. You only have a few seconds to determine which lane you need to be in to head in the right direction. A dimly lit tunnel encloses you, the square tiles on the walls shimmering ever-so-slightly from the lights above that brighten as the tunnel ends.

After some time in the dark abyss, you emerge from the tunnel to reveal an exquisite, breathtaking view that greets you with open arms and fills your heart with pure joy, excitement, and wonder. The scenic skyline and spectacular sites open up opportunities to explore all that awaits you. Finally, you cross a multitude of bridges that enables you to hurdle over any and all barriers that could prevent you from moving forward toward your purpose or destination.

* * *

Based on the depiction above, it would appear I was narrating the expedition through the rolling hills of Western

Pennsylvania and the infamous ride through the Fort Pitt Tunnel going inbound toward Downtown Pittsburgh. This is an experience both residents and first-time visitors of the Steel City get to encounter.

With its unexpected challenges, life mirrors the twists and turns of navigating the Pittsburgh landscape.

WHAT BEFALLS US DURING LIFE'S STORMS

Life is full of ups and downs, highs and lows, and peaks and valleys. Sometimes the path in one's life has rough edges, grooves, and can be unevenly paved; other times the path is smooth and flat for miles on end. The landscape of life consists of summits that have you soaring high above the clouds and bottomless valleys that bring immense, unexpected experiences in our lives. At some point, we will be struck by one or more major derailments that throw our lives into disarray in unpredictable ways. Life's mountainous challenges can be exceedingly difficult to overcome and limit us from fully enjoying all the moments life has to offer.

The challenges we will inevitably face in life that I'm referring to are those that are burdensome, cause confusion, stress, and disorder, and make you question everything and anything about your life and reality. Serious distressing events that can plague our lives include accidents, life-threatening conditions or diagnoses, mental illnesses, surgeries, sudden deaths of loved ones, abuse, harassment, natural disasters, shootings, crimes, economic depressions or recessions, pandemics, and wars. Life-altering challenges such as these will undoubtedly leave lasting imprints and impacts on ourselves, our loved ones, and communities.

Undergoing dramatic, stressful events in life triggers two natural, yet detrimental reactions: trauma and grief. According to the Mental Health Foundation, trauma is the shock response to a distressing or disturbing event related to the risk of serious harm or perception of actual or threatened death. Trauma overwhelms an individual's ability to cope with their unfortunate circumstance and causes feelings of worthlessness and helplessness.[6]

From the outset, trauma alters your thought-processing capabilities and the perceptions of your life, resulting in self-blame, negative self-talk, intrusive flashbacks or triggers, and difficulty making decisions. When experiencing a traumatic event, your body's defenses take effect and create a stress response, making you feel a variety of physical symptoms, behave differently, and express more intense emotions. As a result, your body becomes stuck in this overwhelming "emergency"—or panicked—state, which makes navigating through past or current setbacks difficult.[7]

The other emotional and physical response—grief—refers to the reaction to a loss or to any kind of abrupt change. Grieving is not exclusive to the loss of a loved one through death.

---

6 "The Impact of Traumatic Events on Mental Health," Mental Health Foundation, accessed on March 2, 2020.

7 Substance Abuse and Mental Health Services Administration (SAMHSA), "Chapter 3 Understanding the Impact of Trauma," *Trauma-Informed Care in Behavioral Health Services*, 2014.

The American Counseling Association states that grief is a reaction to the loss of anyone or anything to which an individual is deeply attached to. In unsettling and life-altering circumstances, we might endure a loss of security, normalcy, comfort, motivation, hope, and sense of identity.[8]

Elisabeth Kübler-Ross' five traditional stages of grief—denial, anger, bargaining, depression, and acceptance—still has immense value when coping with any loss. Yet, what has evolved over the years is the comprehension that grief is not a smooth, linear, or predictable process. The stages of grief overlap significantly and are not necessarily followed in any predetermined fashion; instead they're solely driven by each individual's unique way of working through their obstacle in their own time.[9]

In my case, during the initial moments of hearing the news of my father's diagnosis, a thousand questions invaded my mind with no clear answers. I caught myself going downhill on the path toward rock bottom before affirming my decision to live out and believe that my family's traumatic experience would positively transform our lives. Throughout our unexpected circumstance, my family and I strived to patiently heal, talk, listen to our thoughts and feelings, pray, and even cry together.

Trauma and grief encompass a range of feelings that vary in intensity; they can catalyze imposing feelings of guilt, anger,

---

8 Laurie Meyers, "Grief: Going beyond Death and Stages," *Counseling Today, A Publication of the American Counseling Association*, October 27, 2016.

9 Ibid.

regret, rejection, frustration, sadness, self-blame, and confusion. Wrestling with and managing these daunting emotions while reconciling with our distressing experiences is exceedingly difficult, leaving us feeling anxious, uncertain, and lost. Burdensome challenges shatter our preexisting assumptions, fundamental expectations, and deeply rooted beliefs about ourselves, our lives, and reality like fragments of glass.

THE FORMIDABLE VOID OF VICTIMIZATION AND NEGATIVITY

We have a strong, unyielding tendency to spiral down the never-ending vortex of victimization and negativity. Amid life's unsettling situations, people struggle to develop an understanding of how something could have happened and why they were singled out to be a victim. We have a tendency to assess whether there were any cause-and-effect laws governing the universe that can possibly explain why we were chosen as a victim in an attempt to make sense of these unexpected events. When feeling victimized or singled out, we undermine our ability to do anything about our situation. We feel powerless and assume we lack any sense of control in our lives to alter our circumstances.

In an attempt to process and adapt to distressing, unexpected crises, we all struggle to answer the "why" question. As we strive to find any feasible explanation for our obstacles, we shift the blame back and forth between our external environment and ourselves. This toxic mentality also manifests recurring thoughts such as, "Poor me. Why me?" "I'm the only person going through this," and "I failed and there's nothing I can do about it," causing you to pity yourself.[10]

Along my journey, I have found that victimization is a combination of seeing most things in life as negative, believing it's beyond your control, and thinking you deserve better. You see your entire life through a small, narrow, and rigid lens based off of a negative experience and assume bad things constantly happen to you and to you alone.

Negative or unwanted thoughts are fear-based, stemming from our insecurities: the aspects of our life that have wounded us or made us worry. A negative mindset can bog us down and make it hard for us to operate when facing extreme adversities. No matter how hard we try to avoid them, negative thoughts are everywhere, waiting to steer us off track and distract us. We suppress our true thoughts and feelings and struggle to confront our setbacks in healthy approaches.

During my time overcoming life setbacks and learning about other people's stories, I have come to the realization that we have *hardwired* our brains to gravitate to *negativity*. Negative and stressful events have a greater impact on our brains than positive ones, which explains why past traumas can have prolonged and lingering effects, why we're more likely to notice the negative things, and why we tend to dwell upon or remember negative events more vividly.

---

10 Debra Kaminer and Gillian Eagle, "Trauma as a Crisis of Meaning," In *Traumatic Stress in South Africa*, 60–79, (Johannesburg, South Africa: Wits University Press, 2010).

According to HR Manager and Positive Psychology expert Catherine Moore, negativity bias refers to our tendency to give more psychological weight and importance to all things bad rather than good. A negative outlook on your life can make you perceive the worst and think your life will never get better. Heavy, challenging moments tend to shape us, but automatically defaulting to negativity keeps the experience trapped in our hearts and minds, preventing us from letting it go and moving on. [11]

Avoiding the situation altogether and admitting defeat to your circumstances will keep you deeply grounded at the bottom of the valley.

If you continually have a pessimistic outlook on your circumstances, you will invoke a domino effect of consequences that can impede your ability to overcome these setbacks and live a fulfilling life. The American Psychological Association found that common initial reactions associated with singular, multiple, or enduring distressing events fall across the emotional, physical, cognitive, and behavioral domains. Beyond the initial emotional reactions during the event, feelings of anger, fear, shame, and depression are most likely to surface, leading one to feeling irritable, fragile, numb, and detached. Physical symptoms that can manifest over time include sleep disturbances, fatigue, and impaired immune system.[12]

---

11 Catherine Moore, "What Is the Negativity Bias and How Can It Be Overcome?" *Positive Psychology*, March 8, 2020.

12 Kevin Rowell and Rebecca Thomley, "Recovering Emotionally from Disaster," *American Psychological Association*, 2013.

In addition to these short-term effects, prolonging your comeback from your temporary setback will result in chronic stress, lasting for several months or even years. Unhealthy coping mechanisms like substance and drug abuse, irritability or angry outbursts, and negative self-talk or suicidal thinking can falter your progress toward recovery. Exposure to severe traumatic events can result in significant and long-term symptoms such as post-traumatic stress disorder (PTSD), depression, eating disorders, anxiety, and any long-term health effects impairing the heart, liver, autoimmune, respiratory, and neurological systems. Those who are experiencing any of the extreme consequences like PTSD or other severe mental health issues should get additional help as needed.[13]

BEYOND THE MEANS OF SIMPLY SURVIVING

Succumbing to your circumstances can leave you in shock and suffering for years to come. The inability to overcome your setbacks not only impedes numerous aspects of your well-being, but can also halt your own existential or personal development. You may not get to choose your circumstances, but you ultimately decide how they impact you, what outlook on life you will embrace, and how you will grow from your experiences.

A psychological debriefing from the United States Substance Abuse and Mental Health Services Administration found

13 SAMHSA, *Trauma-Informed Care in Behavioral Health Services,* 2014.

that overwhelming stress and uncertainty can convince us our lives have become meaningless. Life-altering obstacles affect one's perceptions about the future by means of losing hope, having limited expectations about life, fearing they don't have much longer left to live, or anticipating that normal life events won't occur.[14]

Obstructions and barriers can only do two things: stop us in our tracks or force us to get creative, become innovative, learn, and grow from the experiences, and turn things around for the better.

Our challenges do not have to be viewed as destructive and detrimental. Many people have experienced traumatic events and have prevailed to live a fulfilling life. Instead of looking at our challenges and limitations as something negative, we need to begin perceiving them as magnificent gifts and catalysts that ignite our drive and passions, helping us go further than anyone ever thought possible and see what amazing opportunities are in store for us.

Living beyond our limits may appear to be a dream or a figment of our imagination, but that is not the case.

In 1962, doctors diagnosed Stephen Hawking, a twenty-one-year-old student acquiring his PhD at Cambridge

---

14 Ibid.

University, with a degenerative motor neuron disease and predicted a life expectancy of about two years. Despite this diagnosis, Hawking became the world's leading theoretical physicist and cosmologist by explaining the intersections of gravity and quantum mechanics. He lived to be sevety-six years old.[15]

How did he accomplish all that?

Ryan Shazier, a former linebacker for the Pittsburgh Steelers and the Ohio State University, sustained a spinal contusion and had only a 20 percent chance of walking again. However, he managed to not only recover but to continue demonstrating leadership on the sidelines, thrive in his personal life, and view his injury as a blessing.[16]

How did he accomplish all that?

Gabby Giffords, a former member of the United States House of Representatives, was shot in the head in an assassination attempt outside of Tucson, Arizona in January 2011. Despite this traumatic event, she continually works through her ongoing recovery, has become a public advocate for gun control, and believes her brain injury allowed her to move ahead as a better, stronger, and tougher individual.[17]

How did she accomplish all that?

---

15 "Biography," Stephan Hawking, accessed March 16, 2020.

16 Bryan DeArdo, "Ryan Shazier Celebrates His Continued Recovery on Two-Year Anniversary of Spinal Injury," *CBS Sports,* December 6, 2019.

17 Gabby Giffords and Mark Kelly, "The New Year Is a Time for Hope, Even after Tragedy," *Time*, November 30, 2017.

What do Stephan Hawking, Ryan Shazier, and Gabby Giffords have in common?

We all have the capability of going beyond merely surviving our circumstances and thriving in them. The ways we learn to cope with the worst things in life can give us amazing new capabilities, outlooks, and opportunities to live out our meaningful life purpose(s).

These capabilities and outlook include the eight building blocks and the continuous growth mindset, which will be explored in the next chapter.

CHAPTER 4

EMPOWERING INSIGHTS

When faced with extreme adversities, stressors, and uncertainties, it's hard to imagine proclaiming that these can be great moments in our lives, welcoming them as gifts, and seeing them as occasions to learn more about ourselves and our purpose. Yet, many of the beautiful, precious, and transformational things in our lives come at the end of difficult seasons or after weathering life's storms.

Challenges are natural—do not beat yourself up over the difficulties you may experience or the challenges life throws your way. Having a rewarding life does not mean having no challenges; it's about navigating challenges with conscious awareness, becoming empowered to overcome and learn from them, and prioritizing your personal growth. Things can become wonderful in life when we overcome, prevail, and learn during dark times. Whether it be an illness, job loss, natural disaster, or unexpected death, we all have within us the capability to spark marvelous transformations from seemingly negative experiences.

We all can grow beyond life's moments.

> Continuously growing beyond life's moments is about opening your heart, mind, and soul to learning, persevering, and discovering your true potential after surmounting life's mountainous challenges.

The concept of going beyond your circumstances recognizes that life is full of difficulties, yet there is a "beyond" that exists and an abundance of opportunities that await you that will help you discover your purpose in life. Each challenge you overcome is a part of your life's journey, continually moving you forward and away from dwelling on the past.

This novel outlook on how we can perceive our challenges provides clear insight on how myself and countless others did not merely survive our life-altering challenges—we flourished in the midst of the adversities in our lives. To further illustrate how to transform your setbacks into your greatest comebacks, let us revisit and examine Stephan Hawking, Ryan Shazier, and Gabby Giffords.

THE TRIUMPHS BEHIND LIFE'S TRIALS

STEPHEN HAWKING

In 1962, Stephen Hawking was diagnosed with degenerative motor neuron disease, a condition that quickly robs individuals of the ability to voluntarily move their muscles. He experienced progressively disabling effects, losing all abilities except for those in the brain, and had a life expectancy of two years. Faced with this life-altering disease, Hawking stayed resilient and wasted no time pursuing his passions and careers as a theoretical physicist, cosmologist, and space traveler. In 1974, Hawking outlined his theory that black holes emit "Hawking radiation" and investigated the beginning of time, proving the universe began in a singularity, according to general relativity.[18] Hawking also led a fulfilling personal life—he married Jane Wilde and had three children with her.

Hawking thrived beyond his condition to become one of the most famous scientists in the world. His book, *A Brief History of Time*, has sold more than 10 million copies since its publication in 1988. He has received over a dozen honorary degrees, some of them include Commander of the British Empire in 1982, Companion of Honor in 1989, the Copley Medal from the Royal Society in 2006, and the U.S. Presidential Medal of Freedom in 2009. Queen Elizabeth II also offered Hawking a knighthood in the late 1990s. Perhaps one of Hawking's biggest accomplishments is surpassing his life expectancy by fifty-four years.[19]

RYAN SHAZIER

Ryan Shazier was a first-time All-American, selected for the First-Team All-Big Ten Conference football team in 2013 and competed in two Pro Bowls in 2016 and 2017. His career with the Pittsburgh Steelers began in 2014 upon forging his

18 Stephan Hawking, *My Brief History* (United Kingdom: Bantam Books, 2013), 3–121.

19 Ibid.

senior season at the Ohio State University. On December 4, 2017, Shazier sustained a severe back injury after a head-on tackle during a Monday Night Football game against the Cincinnati Bengals. This injury proved to become one of the worst injuries to ever air on live television. Sustaining a spinal contusion during the prime years of his football career that left him with barely a 20 percent chance of walking again was not a part of Ryan Shazier's life plans. Despite his injury and absence from the 2018 and 2019 seasons, Shazier continually rose above his circumstances to see what awaited him in his life beyond his derailment. After aggressive rehabilitation, Shazier was not only able to walk again but could run, and his fellow peers ranked him on the NFL's Top 100 Players list in 2018.[20]

Shazier continues to be a part of the Steelers organization, leading and mentoring both on and off the sidelines by participating in daily workouts, scouting college players, attending coaches' meetings, and learning about the financial side of the professional sports industry. In addition to these significant contributions to the Steelers, Shazier earned his masters' degree in business from the University of Pittsburgh and took part in several business ventures. Shazier also received the 2019 George Halas Award from the Professional Football Writers of America, which is awarded to an NFL player, coach, or staff member who overcame adversity to succeed. On September 9, 2020, Shazier announced his NFL retirement. During the press conference, he shared with his fans that he wanted to explore

---

20 Rob Todor, "Ryan Shazier to Present Inspirational Story of Recovery at Record-Courier's Best of Preps Event," *Record-Courier,* June 6, 2019.

God's purpose for him beyond leaving his mark on the sport of football. [21]

GABBY GIFFORDS

Gabby Giffords served in Arizona's state Congress for four years, from 2001 to 2005, becoming the third woman and the youngest woman in Arizona's history to be elected. Additionally, she served as a member of the United States House of Representatives from 2007 to 2012, representing Arizona's eighth congressional district. In 2007, she married former U.S. Navy captain and NASA astronaut, Captain Mark Kelly.

In January 2011, during her third term in Congress, Giffords was shot in the head in an assassination attempt and mass shooting outside of Tucson, Arizona. The bullet wound caused a traumatic brain injury that paralyzed most of the right side of her face. As a result, she lost some peripheral vision and struggled to speak in complete sentences. By August 2011, Giffords' had recovered enough to return to the House floor, where she was greeted with a standing ovation.

The day after President Obama's State of the Union address in January 2012, Giffords formally submitted her resignation.[22] Giffords' injury sparked a new life purpose: she dedicated her life to service, became an ardent advocate for gun control,

---

21 *NFL*, "Pittsburgh Steelers Linebacker Ryan Shazier Talks about His Relentless Recovery," 2019, Video, 6:28; Ryan Shazier (@shazier), "Thank You .....," Instagram video, September 9, 2020.

22 Kathleen McCleary, "Life Is Good: The Story of Mark Kelly and Gabby Giffords," *Parade*, February 10, 2017.

and, with her husband, launched the organization, "Giffords," following the events at Sandy Hook. "Giffords" has led the national gun safety movement, making it a primary issue for voters, supporting gun safety laws, and helping pass significant legislation in both individual states and in the United States House of Representatives. Her husband, Mark Kelly, shared in a TED Talk that Gabby looks ahead every day and tries to figure out how to be a positive force in the world. "She doesn't get down; she realizes we can't go back in time and there's no undoing this. All you can do is try to do the best you can with what you've got." [23]

* * *

All three of these individuals are well-known; many have heard of them before and recognize their greatness, accomplishments, and careers. However, the true reason why I commend, look up to, and appreciate Stephen Hawking, Ryan Shazier, and Gabby Giffords is because they not only have faced and overcome so much but have also thrived throughout and beyond their circumstances.

After my dad's diagnosis, my view of life-changing setbacks evolved to recognize that we all have and will face struggles throughout our lives that can positively shape our futures, careers, passions, and purposes. Through my dad's battle with an extremely rare cancer and other life experiences, I learned that I, too, have the capabilities to overcome something . . . anything . . . we all do!

---

23 *TED*, "Gabby Giffords and Mark Kelly: Be Passionate. Be Courageous. Be Your Best," April 11, 2014, video, 18:48.

THE BEAUTY HIDDEN THROUGHOUT AND BEYOND OUR CIRCUMSTANCES

When we are faced with an unexpected or traumatic obstacle, we typically default to simply surviving it. However, constantly being in survival mode prohibits us from living a wonderful life because we let the hustle and bustle, pain, or distress of our lives completely consume us; it clogs our abilities to think positively, achieve goals, and put our aspirations into motion.

We only have a finite amount of mental, emotional, and physical energy to give our world each day, and constantly fighting against the challenges will only exhaust our energy that's truly meant for creating, living, and being happy. The purpose of life is not to merely survive; it's about thriving in your past or current circumstances and discovering what lies ahead on your journey! Thriving turns your crises or setbacks into transformative opportunities.

Although it was completely unexpected and initially shook me to my core, I believe my dad's diagnosis and recovery from his rare cancer was one of the most extraordinary things to ever happen to me and my family. Throughout the journey and to this day, as I look back on my family's life-altering situation, I cannot help but continually feel overjoyed, express gratification, and respectfully admire my family and our lives. The battle against the tumor made us come together as a family and I am grateful for that lasting closeness.

Furthermore, I am thankful for having a fighting chance to persevere through this setback, to work through my family's cancerous obstacles to shine brightly on the other side. Looking back on my past circumstances, I visibly recognize how various lessons, capabilities, and moments during my derailments led me beyond to enjoy unique opportunities, acquire friendships, and strengthen my values, beliefs, and thoughts.

Cancer taught my dad that he is much stronger than he ever thought he was. Faced with a daunting diagnosis, my dad kept moving forward and living, never giving up or admitting defeat. In the process of his surgery, treatments, and post-recovery, my dad did not just survive—he bloomed in extreme adversity, running laps around his opponent, cancer. He embodied this untouchable mindset that allowed him to be committed to making the most of every day and to become at least 1 percent better than he was the day before. He never lost hope, the will to fight, or his drive to continue living a meaningful life. He also never gave up his role of being my father.

* * *

Finding the good in distressing situations gave me a sense of appreciation for my life and all the opportunities yet to come. Positively transcending obstacles also improved my relationships with others, my perceptions about myself and the surrounding world, caused me to acquire more appreciation for my life's moments, and sparked my greater satisfaction with life. One of the many positive things I discovered when experiencing my family's life-altering setback was unlocking the real meanings of my life.

As I met extraordinary people both personally and professionally, I learned I am not the only one who proactively chooses light over darkness and gravitates toward embodying more positivity than negativity in the midst of their setbacks. Furthermore, all the individuals I interviewed and/or researched stated that their life-altering challenges were one of the best and greatest things that has ever happened to them. They all believe their experiences shaped them into the person they are today and propelled them toward their personal and professional passions.

Challenges give us clarity, reveal our authentic identity and self-worth, and remind us what is inherently important in our lives. Our setbacks are meaningful experiences that can teach us valuable lessons that we can add to our toolkit to draw upon in future situations to support ourselves and others. These pivotal lessons are not necessarily taught within the walls of a classroom or lecture hall; they're intrinsic qualities and capabilities that are acquired, practiced, and reinforced through our life's experiences and challenges.

Throughout the life challenges that Hawking, Shazier, Giffords, myself, and the heroes I interviewed have overcome, there are eight comprehensive lessons that bind our journeys together, serving as building blocks. I learned that when overcoming obstacles, we never start from scratch; we start from previous experiences. The lessons I learned throughout my challenges prepared me for other life moments, allowed me to continually build off of them through all the ups and downs of life, and sparked my transformation to become stronger, wiser, and better. Ultimately, the building blocks propelled me and other individuals forward toward a new understanding and objective in our lives that we're all capable of achieving: continuous growth.

THE JOURNEY AHEAD

If you have the intention of prevailing through your life's unexpected circumstances, the building blocks and continuous growth mindset need to become intricate parts of your life. These building blocks are meant to be learned and used as needed so you can go the distance into the beyond.

You don't stop growing after one day or after surmounting one challenge; real growth is about learning and developing as you hurdle obstacles, then applying the lessons you learned to life, future challenges, and exciting opportunities. Embodying the eight building blocks and the growth mindset will have direct implications on your life. They will not only support you while you navigate and thrive in your life's unexpected circumstances but will also empower you both personally and professionally.

In the upcoming pages of this book, we will embark on a self-growth expedition together. I will reveal what the eight fundamental building blocks are and how myself and my acquaintances leveraged them to overcome our assorted array of challenges. Through the use of interviews, storytelling, and reflections, I will dive further into how striving toward continuous growth can unlock endless opportunities for you to find the passion or purpose that has been tugging at your heart strings.

Follow my lead into the dark, shadowy tunnel as we explore the building blocks while making our way, in strides, toward our objective: a small orb of light that is just waiting for us on the other side.

The beyond.

PART II

THE EIGHT BUILDING BLOCKS

CHAPTER 5

GAINING PERSPECTIVE

"However bad life may seem, there is always something we can do and succeed at. While there's life, there is hope." [24]

—STEPHEN HAWKING

At just nine years old, Anna needed open-heart surgery to address an unexplainable hole that had developed. Anna did not initially grasp the severity of her circumstances until later in life when she was diagnosed with severe depression and anxiety. As Anna got older and learned to hurdle her obstacles, her mentality transformed to perceive her life as a precious gift to be cherished.

"Life is sacred, and you don't know what is always coming your way that can hit you like a ton of bricks," Anna shared with me. "You also don't realize how quickly it can be taken away from you in a manner of seconds."

24 James Marsh, *The Theory of Everything*, (London, England: Working Title Films, 2014), DVD.

Anna became appreciative of all of life's little moments and how they add up to an incredible adventure toward one's purpose. She also recognized how the small speed bumps in her life could be a sign that greater, wonderful, and more exciting things are ahead of her. As she tackled her pent-up issues in therapy, Anna learned how to look at the bigger picture, viewing the world in an unparalleled lens.

"It is difficult to see things mentally in a new light unless something happens to you personally," Anna stated. "If I heard only stories about unfortunate circumstances happening to other people and not truly experiencing them for myself, I don't think it would have affected me as much."

Everything Anna gained from prevailing through her life's biggest challenges was further solidified when she attended a Jesuit university. The school's religious support and emphasis, in addition to the people Anna met along her undergrad journey, enabled her to gain a deeper perspective of life and how it has brought amazing gifts and people into her life.

"The incredible people I met during my collegiate years pushed me to see more through experiences and faith to uncover what I was missing in life. It made me realize that I'm not the only one who feels or thinks this way and reassured me that traumatic experiences can steer me into the direction of making exceptional changes in my life."

Anna doesn't wish to close herself off from anything, especially if things do happen for a reason, nor does she wish her life's biggest challenges away. By being open and receptive to the experiences and people around her, Anna sets a tremendous example for how to work through troubling times, acquire a new perspective by using life's setbacks to find new meaning in life, and strive to continually be the inspiring person you are meant to become.

* * *

Gaining perspective allows you to change the meaning of your life's circumstances, comprehend your emotions, and take appropriate action to move forward—it governs your entire outlook on life. Acquiring a new perspective on your life and circumstances requires you to trust where you are and how you got here; realistic perspectives of yourself and the world provide you with a sense of insight and closure. Embodying a novel perspective on your life's setbacks requires you to recognize that our life challenges and stressors are merely temporary speed bumps or hiccups rather than impossible problems that cannot be solved.

Going through any kind of tragedy, dilemma, or loss can serve as a transformational moment; it can awaken you from an unconscious state of being so you can fully appreciate life with all its ups and downs. When you have a broader picture of life and adjust your lens, you are able to connect to something beyond your own circumstances knowing that an abundance of good can stem from your struggles.

A zoomed-out perspective on life gives you a refreshed mindset when overcoming obstacles: what you're currently facing or working through today could perhaps be the very thing that prepares you to change the world tomorrow and in the future.

Gaining perspective allows you to come to terms with knowing life's greatest challenges don't happen to one person alone. This is probably one of the hardest things to truly realize. Although we feel like we're the only ones experiencing loss, grief, suffering, fear, or stress, that's certainly not the case. What adds to internalizing our struggles is believing we will never cross paths with others who have stepped in our shoes, walked their own similar paths to ours, or truly comprehend what it's like to deal with and overcome difficult times.

The truth is, we do indeed cross paths with others who can understand the uncertain times we have been through; however, it took adequate time and patience for me to arrive at this realization.

Although I received numerous words of encouragement and prayers from neighbors, family, and close friends, I still felt remarkably alone when faced with my dad's ever-evolving diagnosis and recovery. At the time, I was fortunate to have lived in a protected, sheltered, bubble-like community until the age of eighteen when I went to college.

Or so I thought.

My community was overprotective; the privileged life within my wealthy community had skewed my definition of reality. Out there in the beyond, countless hardships were a natural part of families, communities, suburbs, and cities. Life-altering circumstances, such as my family's, were unheard of in my town where mansion-sized homes were visible across the rolling hills, families owned more than three cars, and girls in high school carried Michael Kors purses as backpacks.

My community partially failed me because they closed themselves off from the rest of the world and threw away the key. Stuck in this enclosure, I didn't know other people were battling cancer and working through other exceedingly difficult challenges like my family's.

All I wanted to know was that I wasn't alone in how I was thinking, feeling, or navigating my circumstances. I yearned for someone—*anyone*—who walked a comparable journey to mine and knew what it was like to have to mature and grow up at the age of fifteen because your childhood had abruptly ended. I wanted to talk to someone who understood how challenging it was to deal with these circumstances in the midst of high school drama that lingered in every classroom, hallway, and square inch of the building.

* * *

As it turns out, the bubble eventually did pop for me, dissipating my loneliness along with it. In late April 2012, my family received more unfortunate news about my dad's recovery. Seeing how my family's circumstances were impeding my attitude, happiness, and athletic abilities, I decided to finally share with my lacrosse team the trials I was facing at home.

During one afternoon practice, I stood up in the middle of our group huddle as the rest of my teammates sat on the turf field getting sock tans from the afternoon sun. Over the course of several deep breaths, long pauses, and swallowed tears, I shared my story, leaving no dry eyes in the audience. As my last sentence broke through the humid air, I received a swarm of embraces from my teammates.

After our team huddle, I went over to get a drink of water at the bench before our scrimmages started. As I wiped the sweat and water off my face, one of my teammates, Olivia, approached me.

"Hey Nicole! Listen . . . I . . . I feel terrible about what is happening to you and your family. My mom, she had a cancer too, but I was a little younger." Olivia paused for a brief moment and then continued, out of earshot from our fellow teammates.

"Everything happens for reason. Looking back over the last several years, I saw how everything does and has fallen into place, one way or another. Overcoming my family's circumstances got me to where I am today, and I wouldn't want to be anywhere else."

As Olivia spoke, I found the living proof I had been missing since January. I was not the only one who was committed to the mindset that everything that's good will manifest itself through these troubling times. I stood in awe as I absorbed each and every word.

"High school is difficult enough without overcoming a family struggle like yours. No one deserves to go through that alone."

Olivia took a deep, calming breath and resumed. "It is hard when someone is going through a tough time but doesn't have the outlet to talk about it, especially because I went through something similar yet very different."

Olivia read me like a book, knowing exactly how I felt and what I needed to hear as she turned the pages of my life over the past few months.

"I'm here for you, if you need anything or want to talk."

"Ah, thank you, Olivia," I replied wholeheartedly, beaming with joy. A sense of peace and comfort washed over me. "You have no idea how much your support and perspective mean to me."

Olivia smiled back and wrapped her arm around my shoulder, escorting me to center field.

"Come on, we got a game to win tomorrow!"

Olivia and I were in the same grade and we had played lacrosse together since we were in fifth grade. However, that was the first real conversation I had with her. It must not have been easy for Olivia to share that personal information with me, yet it made all the difference in the world to me. She was the first person to openly share her experience with me, to know what recurring emotions and thoughts I had, and to confirm everything does work itself out in the end even better than before.

As Olivia and I walked side-by-side onto the field, I felt this enormous pressure being lifted off my shoulders. Our conversation instilled within me the importance of momentarily shifting my focus away from my circumstances to clearly hear other people's stories. Shifting my perspective to place myself in Olivia's shoes as she dealt with her mom's battle with cancer served as a productive, meaningful reflection. This intentional exercise illustrated to me that I, too, am capable of overcoming this setback to find fulfillment and opportunities ahead on my life's journey. More importantly, I learned I should never feel alone when faced with an overwhelming setback or distress.

According to research conducted by University of California, Berkeley, one of the most effective means of taking a step back and viewing your circumstances more objectively is by acquiring a self-distanced perspective. This productive and progressive approach to discerning your experiences creates opportunities to freely discuss your difficult event, make better sense of your reactions, and experience less emotional distress and physical stress.[25]

As Olivia shared her experiences regarding her mom's past battle with cancer, not only did I personally relate to every conflicting thought or emotion with which she was burdened, but I also gained clarity about my own family's circumstances. What I was thinking, feeling, and going through was not unique to me—it's what bound us closer together.

* * *

Following this insightful moment on the turf field, I gradually felt more at ease and content with my circumstances. I

---

25 Amy L. Eva, "Four Ways to Gain Perspective on Negative Events," *Greater Good Magazine*, September 12, 2017.

continually strove to find affirmations that there was happiness, positivity, and life beyond the pain and trauma. I finally had a role model to look up to as an inspiration that proved there's an end to the ominous tunnel.

Gaining perspective regarding my family's derailment sparked my interest in wanting to meet and talk to cancer survivors. I wanted to hear their stories, put myself in their shoes, and find more ways to view my life-altering setback as transformative rather than detrimental.

Fortunately, my wish came true.

It was the first Saturday of June and the last weekend before school officially ended for the summer. My neighbors, the Carters, invited me to attend the Relay for Life celebration at my high school stadium. The Carters had attended this celebration each year since Mr. Carter survived his battle with cancer several years ago.

When we strode up the worn-out concrete incline that led up to the entrance of the stadium, the track and turf field was covered with illuminating candles in colorful paper bags, soaring balloons, large tents, and live music. About a hundred people gathered at the fifty-yard line near where our mascot was printed on the field in white and red. As we approached the center of the field, the coordinator of the event spoke over the loudspeaker.

"Thank you all for joining us today to celebrate the days, birthdays, moments, and lives of cancer survivors. Would our heroic survivors please join me as we prepare to walk our lap of victory?"

Emerging from the crowd, thirty people, including Mr. Carter, made their way toward the announcer. They represented a variety of ages: the elderly, baby boomers, teenagers, and children. As the survivors lined up to start their walk, the crowd roared with applause, cries of joy, and screams of intense pride. I gazed at this spectacle . . . this moment of underlying truth, perspective, and discovery brought me to tears as I joined the crowd in cheering on these survivors.

As I watched the survivors, a powerful image appeared in my mind. On the track, I envisioned my father standing next to Mr. Carter and the other survivors. At the sound of a whistle, I could witness my dad walking, jogging, and eventually running effortlessly. From afar, I could see the bright smirk on his face, catch him waving at me the way he does on his runs. His eyes would look at me, piercing my heart and triggering the onset of tears and emotions flooding within me. To think my father, possibly next year, could be here walking his lap of victory in celebration among other cancer survivors was an extraordinary realization.

The Relay for Life celebration was a sign that wonderful and positive aspects of life awaited me and my family throughout and after my dad's diagnosis. It served as a humbling reminder that my dad would beat the cancer, become a survivor, recover, and find a new normal. My family was going to be okay. I was going to be okay. Attending this celebration with the Carter family, witnessing the celebratory walk, and meeting so many survivors of all ages further reinforced the importance of looking at life with a new perspective.

* * *

Whether we realize it or not, we are surrounded by clear testimonies of those who have thrived throughout and beyond life's challenges. The two moments on the turf field reinforced my appreciation for the true value of my life experiences, both traumatic and uplifting. By taking a step back and viewing the lives of Olivia, the Carters, and scores of other individuals, I acquired realistic and optimistic perspectives amid my current circumstances. This novel perspective shined light on the fact that no matter what we are dealing with, we are never alone. Our challenges are just a piece of the larger puzzle that make our life meaningful and ignite real growth.

Taking on a new perspective began with opening my eyes, heart, and mind to discover all the intricate, intertwining pieces that make up my life's journey. I realized I did not necessarily have to be looking over the Grand Canyon or standing out on the Willis Tower's Skydeck glass balcony to obtain a new vantage point on my life and temporary setbacks. I can look at my life right now from ten thousand feet. I simply must adjust my focus from looking inward to zooming out; this allows me to connect to other's stories. By learning from other people and how their challenges positively impacted their lives, I will continue to build ever-lasting bridges that carry beyond my setbacks.

CHAPTER 6

VULNERABILITY AND TRANSPARENCY

"Life is about to get tough.
You're allowed to be angry.
You're allowed to be sad.
You're allowed to be hurt.
And it may never seem like it, but this pain is a gift. Because when you're ready, you'll turn all of that pain into something incredible. It will become light to the world. Promise."

—RAVEN M.

Reoccurring, horrible headaches prompted Nick to visit the doctor. Initially, a CAT scan revealed he had a traumatic brain injury, but after being sent for an MRI, the doctors discovered a tumor. The probable prognosis was that the tumor must have formed when Nick was born and linked to his condition—cortical dysplasia—where developing brain cells fail to reach their genetically destined parts of the brain.

Nick spent countless months having regular MRI scans to ensure the tumor was not growing in any sensitive spots. Unfortunately, during the summer before his sophomore year of high school, Nick experienced more intense pain. While traveling and playing competitive golf, he could barely finish a round without getting horrible vertigo, migraines, double vision, and muscle spasms. A few weeks later, an MRI scan made an unexpected discovery: the tumor had quadrupled in size at a rate the doctors had never seen before.

On August 6, 2013, Nick underwent an eight-hour surgery. He was hospitalized for six days and dealt with excruciating pain for the next two months. The most profound change that Nick experienced after the doctors removed his tumor was his personality; the tumor was located near the amygdala, the area of the brain that coordinates and triggers our emotional responses like anger, fear, sadness, and anxiety.

"Before the surgery, I was an outgoing person and never shy. I liked meeting new people and never was super anxious or paranoid," Nick recollected during our interview. "Within the first year after the tumor was removed, I felt isolated and acquired social anxiety; it's something that I'm still dealing with today."

After the surgery, Nick noticed how people asked him if they could do things for him or if they could help him with something. Nick was initially upset that people offered him help—he didn't want his family and friends to treat him differently because of his surgery. Although it takes time to recover and find a new sense of normalcy again, Nick knew he had to be upfront and lower his emotional defenses. Opening up eased the pain and distress Nick endured from his unfortunate circumstance and enabled him to articulate to his support systems how he felt about his diagnosis and recovery.

"The biggest thing, especially when talking to your doctors, family, and support systems, is that you got to tell them how you feel. Don't leave anything out or ever feel like you're being selfish!" exclaimed Nick. "The only way someone can help you is if you are willing to be open and honest about what you are thinking, feeling, and experiencing."

To this day, Nick continually goes the distance to achieve academic success in his collegiate years and embrace his competitive drive. He redefines what it means to always be working on becoming the best version of yourself. Furthermore, Nick realizes how embracing vulnerability about his thoughts and feelings about his surgery and ongoing recovery made him be open, honest, and transparent with himself and his loved ones.

* * *

Vulnerability is consistently an overlooked trait and perhaps the hardest to fully embrace. According to Dr. Brené Brown, vulnerability is basically uncertainty, weaknesses, emotional exposure, and discomfort. Being vulnerable is generally associated with being frightened, powerless, unprotected, and exposed. We tend to cover up our weaknesses, imperfections, and emotions; however, vulnerability leverages your capability to heal your fractured parts, instills your courage to show up, and helps you be seen and heard when we have no control over uncertain circumstances. [26]

We can't keep pretending, hiding, or denying how we're feeling; instead, we need to acknowledge and embrace our emotions by lowering our protective shields. Emerging from behind the mask and protective armor allows us to be transparent with others. Transparency breeds trust, loyalty, openness, and honesty. If we lean into and embrace vulnerability and transparency, we will be greeted with an abundance of love, trust, joy, and a sense of belonging. Those who embrace their stories full of triumphs and trials believe what made them vulnerable and transparent made them beautiful and genuinely themselves; it allowed them to be seen and feel worthy, enabling the establishment of connections with others.

Coincidentally, both my dad and I had defining moments when we became vulnerable, transparent, and honest toward each other during our family's battle with cancer.

The first moment occurred on Sunday, February 12 at the hospital, which was two days after my dad's surgery. When I visited him in the hospital, he was always in constant pain and hardly spoke at all. He had several IVs hooked up to him, needed the packing in his nose and around his head replaced every hour, and could barely keep down any fluids or food.

---

26 TEDx, "Brené Brown: The Power of Vulnerability," June 1, 2010, video, 20:19.

When visiting, I occupied a chair in one of the back corners of my dad's room, attempting to catch up on reading *Antigone* from *The Theban Plays* for homework. In reality, I was pretending to read, distracted by keeping tabs on my dad despite being afraid to look at him. His suffering was unbearable. I refused to leave my seat for the duration of that weekend, fearful something would happen to my father if I were not there.

That afternoon, as the Pittsburgh Penguins game played on the television, a nurse brought in my dad's lunch from the cafeteria: green beans, macaroni and cheese, and a cup of chocolate pudding. I had hardly eaten anything for the last two days and I eyed the chocolate pudding longingly—it happened to be one of my favorite desserts at the time.

As I heard the horn blare on the televised hockey game, signaling the end of a period, a familiar yet scratchy voice broke the silence.

"Go ahead, sweetheart. Have it." My father's eyes were open as he propped himself up, looking toward the ominous back corner of his room that I had inhabited for the last thirty-six hours. He gestured toward the chocolate pudding on the lunch tray by his bedside.

I shook my head in pure embarrassment. "No . . . Dad, I can't have part of your meal because you need . . ." but my father cut me off mid-sentence.

"Please. For me? It will go to waste . . . It will make me feel better knowing you at least ate something." He sounded desperate, yet so certain this, of all things, would relieve some of his enduring pain.

I slowly got up, using the armrest to support my weight as I regained my balance after sitting in an uncomfortable chair for too long. I walked the few steps to where my father was resting. As I cautiously picked up the glass cup of chocolate pudding and the metal spoon beside it, my dad spoke again through his parched throat.

"I'm sorry I put you through this."

Our eyes met and I saw a single tear fall from his eye and down his left cheek.

I was frozen; I did not know what to say. To avoid my dad seeing me cry, I went back to my seat and quietly ate the chocolate pudding as requested, attempting to enjoy it as I forced down every swallow. Instead, I was holding back tears. It was a horrible feeling. I have not been able to eat chocolate pudding since that day.

Of all people, my dad should have never felt sorry for this circumstance. It was out of his—or anyone's—control and it was no one's fault. Yet, I saw regret, guilt, and sadness wash over his face, feeling ashamed to have to admit his true thoughts and feelings to his only daughter.

At the hospital, my dad was awake, attentive, and alert despite having hardly any strength left and remained silent in the reclining bed. When my dad shared his thoughts with me, it opened both of our hearts. He expressed genuine honesty toward me by telling me how he felt sorry for me during our trying time. Meanwhile, this moment made me realize that although I couldn't fathom what my dad was thinking, feeling, or physically going through, I knew I wanted to stay committed throughout his recovery and patiently listen to what was on his mind.

When we acquire vulnerability, transparency, and a deeper comprehension of ourselves, we can portray ourselves honestly to allow loved ones and their support to come flooding in. Your support systems are there for you, attentively listening to what you may be feeling or thinking; they are patient and committed to have you persevere through your difficult journey. We tend to underestimate the help we truly need, and we should accept every offer for help we receive. It takes a village to get through hard times, and if you do not tell others how they can help you, you won't be able to receive any help at all.

* * *

Vulnerability and transparency go hand-in-hand; you can't have one without the other because they're what connects us to one another the most. When you experience a traumatic event or lose a part of yourself, it is important to talk about it, feel whatever you want to feel, and take the right steps toward feeling better. I learned it is okay to feel something, to express my emotions, and to not always be bulletproof or flawless. I should not beat myself up or feel like I'm failing. If I continued to deny, hide, or push aside my feelings, it could prevent me from seizing new opportunities in my life.

To move forward beyond the pain or distress to receive love and joy, I needed to let vulnerability and transparency mend my wounds.

Unveiling my true feelings to my dad about his cancer diagnosis and healing my wounds involved writing a book. I took the elective course, "Exploring Children's Literature" during my freshman year because I wanted some quality time to devote to writing, or at the very least, to learn about it. Around the middle of March 2012, Mrs. Delaney, the instructor, assigned our final project: writing a children's book. I had no clue what to write about. I was not in the mood to write about butterfly gardens or discovering magical worlds in a closet. After a few days of in-class workshop sessions, Mrs. Delaney noticed I was the only student with nothing written. One day on my way to the next period, she stopped me at the threshold of her classroom.

"Miss Spindler, why haven't you started working on your story?" She tilted her head toward me.

"Honestly, Mrs. Delaney? I do not know what to write about … that is, at the very least, about a happy subject. All I think about all the time is my dad," I genuinely replied.

A puzzling, deep-in-thought look glazed over Mrs. Delaney's face.

"Perhaps," she started to say, "you could write about your situation."

I looked at her with a dumbfounded expression.

"Come again? I don't quite understand..."

"You should write about your family's recent experiences for the audience of children readers, as long as you are comfortable with sharing your story," Mrs. Delaney elaborated. "Your story could be a tool, resource, and comforting support for children and families struggling with similar circumstances and could impact their lives for the better."

I had never thought about how my life could transform the lives of others. I loved the idea and thought it would be a good way for me to let everything out—to release the stress and pressures of my day-to-day life onto the crisp, blank pages of a book.

"I think that idea could work. I'll give it a try," I replied.

Throughout the remainder of the school year, I worked tirelessly to finish the book, putting all my thoughts and emotions into my writing. As the final days of the school year approached, I submitted the assignment. Mrs. Delaney was proud of my accomplishments and gave me an outstanding grade the moment I finished reading my story in front of my class.

After presenting my book, I thought it would be a lovely idea to give the book to my dad for Father's Day. The moment I would read and share this book with my dad would be the first time we would have a real conversation since I heard the unfortunate news six months before; since my dad's recovery prevented him from enjoying daily activities, he lacked the energy to engage in our family conversations. Initially, I was scared to share this book with him—I did not know what he would think of the words I had written or the sketches I had drawn that took me countless hours. This book would expose to my dad my true emotions and thoughts that I had kept bottled up during these difficult times.

Witnessing my dad unintentionally disengage from family life was upsetting. I wanted to lift his spirits up, but I could only imagine the level of pain and discomfort he was experiencing while he healed. I missed having real conversations with my dad, watching the Pittsburgh Penguins hockey games with him, playing catch outside, and being caught in his warm embraces. I hoped this book into which I poured my heart, sweat, and tears would help the two of us grow closer together.

* * *

On Father's Day of 2012, I found my dad getting some fresh air on our patio as the sun was beginning to set on the horizon. With my book in hand, I approached my dad and asked, "Can I join you?"

"Sure, sweetheart." I pulled up a chair beside him, clasping the book close to my chest.

"I have a gift for you for Father's Day. It isn't much, but I want you to listen, okay?"

He nodded his head in reply. I placed the book between us and read the story aloud. I focused on pronouncing each word precisely and slowing down at the proper moments to divulge intense emotions or thoughts. As I finished the last sentence, I turned to look at my dad, who was teary-eyed. He did not try to wipe away the tears as they gushed down his face.

My dad looked at me, his green-gray eyes sparkling.

"Can I have this?" he asked through tears and a slight tremble in his voice.

"It is meant for you. It's our story." I handed him the book and he gripped the cover tightly.

"Thank you! This is the best Father's Day," he said, beaming with immense joy.

I jumped out of the chair and embraced him, carefully avoiding his bandages. That moment made me appreciate not only how much I loved my dad, but also how having the courage to cast our invisibility cloaks off our emotions and thoughts made our father-daughter relationship infinitely stronger. Writing the children's book for my class taught me to be more vulnerable and transparent with my dad. It allowed the light to shine on my pain and wounds, established self-awareness toward myself and others, and made it easier to address my family's setback head-on.

My dad was relieved after allowing himself to become vulnerable with me when he blamed himself for the family's situation. Over the years, he has become more comfortable with being transparent about his thoughts and emotions toward me, mom, and Corey. Being vulnerable allowed my dad and I to get rid of any pent-up baggage with which we were burdened that kept our wall-like barriers up. Through our cancerous derailment, my dad and I definitely reinforced our trust, strengthened our father-daughter bond, and embraced more joy, love, and happiness in our lives. Furthermore, we recognized that we could not progress to the next stage or grow beyond our circumstances without being vulnerable and transparent with ourselves and others.

* * *

Being raw, open, and brave enough to reveal our real thoughts, feelings, and intentions will put our mind, body, soul, and heart at ease. It grants us the capability to face our challenges feeling more comfortable to admit how we feel and what is happening within ourselves. It gives us more control over our pain and scars.

Vulnerability and transparency are intricate pieces to overcoming obstacles and helping us seize all the good things headed our way. By being vulnerable and transparent, you are not only reinforcing a foundation of openness, trust, and clarity, but you are also paving a future that will yield better outcomes from your life's challenging moments.

CHAPTER 7

RESILIENCY

"Life will never give you anything you can't handle." [27]

—JOEL DE CARTERET

Embarking on a year-long journey to recover from a blood disease at age eleven was a derailment that led Addison off the unbeaten path. Her diagnosis evolved her life experiences and transformed her worldview at a much faster pace than a child usually matures. Yet, Addison was set on being resilient throughout her treatments and recovery and became very intentional about seeing this experience as a short-lived twist in her family's much longer life path.

Following her diagnosis, Addison couldn't continue attending public school for the remainder of the year, so her mom and elementary school teacher homeschooled her, which made it exceedingly difficult for her to make new friends

27 Oleg Lougheed, "Life Won't Give You Anything You Can't Handle | Joel de Carteret," July 23, 2018, in *Overcoming Odds Podcast*, podcast, MP3 audio, 49:21.

and maintain old relationships. Despite her circumstances, Addison acquired renewed strength to regain control over her life and persevere through her treatments. Her dad found and implemented therapies to support her immune system so she could engage in activities and bring a sense of normalcy back into her life. While Addison did experience painful treatments, her familial support combined with their ability to afford outside care expedited the pernicious symptoms.

"It is truly freeing to know that your suffering isn't in isolation," Addison told me. "You have to live and work through the challenges, and then you just have to live your life."

Addison pushed her boundaries to be socially engaged and creative during her illness by exploring new hobbies and interests that she still takes part in today. Horseback-riding, exploring nature, painting, and yoga became a part of her identity and ingrained in her heart. Getting into hobbies and connecting with people to work through the uncertain moments of her life strengthened Addison's resilience.

"I found that resiliency comes from understanding that your problem may be the biggest challenge in your own life, but it's definitely not the biggest problem in the world."

Addison acknowledged how continually striving toward having fulfillment in her life allowed her to acquire internal peace and happiness rather than letting her illness define the rest of her life. Overcoming personal challenges opened Addison's eyes and heart to see that she did not have to search far to find that her happiness and strength already existed within her.

"It is important to acknowledge moments, events, and people for what they are and keep moving forward," Addison stated. "What will ultimately allow you to regain control of your immediate situation is trusting yourself and committing to be being better and stronger than you were before."

* * *

Addison's story sets a precedent for how resiliency can help us cope with the curve balls life throws us. Being resilient grants you a sense of control because your thoughts and feelings influence the outcome of your challenge; it involves bouncing back stronger than before from your difficult experiences. Highly resilient people learn how to navigate the rough seas that life's challenges bring, find opportunities to heal, and gradually progress forward to profoundly grow in the face of and beyond adversities, trauma, and stress.

Resilience sparks your comeback story.
Resiliency transforms you from being
the victim to a survivor.
It crowns you the victor of your life.

Dr. Michael Ungar, the Co-Director of the Resiliency Research Centre (RRC) has defined resiliency as an individual's ability to overcome adversity and continue their normal development. To embrace and reinforce resiliency, we need the capacity to find resources—psychological, social, cultural, and physical—that bolster well-being and positively benefits us in meaningful ways. Resiliency can transform our difficulties into learning moments, help us stay committed to our goals, relationships, and beliefs, and makes us feel empowered and confident.[28]

I cannot think of a single time my dad did not exemplify resiliency as he navigated through his traumatic diagnosis and recovery.

He never questioned why or resisted walking blindly beside his medical professionals into the unknown. He hardly ever got angry, frustrated, or discouraged no matter how many times we received unpleasant news. My dad was the pure blend of persistence, resilience, and relentlessness; he wanted to see the sun rise the next day and to beat the living daylights out of cancer by running circles around it. He didn't want to quit because he knew if he kept putting one foot in front of the other, chose not to be negative, and focused on what he wanted, he would realize what he is truly capable of.

Not once did my dad fall victim to the fear that he would never get better as he was recovering at the hospital, sitting through several hours of radiation each day for several weeks, or laying on the recliner chair in the sunroom for six consecutive months post-surgery. He also did not succumb to the tricks and games that cancer can play on the mind. The resiliency my dad had was not only intense, but also consistent and contagious.

A spark of my dad's resiliency imprinted itself on my heart on the day I learned about my dad's diagnosis when I firmly

28 "About Us," Resilience Research Centre, accessed August 23, 2020.

became committed to turn our life-altering experience into something positively worthwhile. My begin-with-the-end-in-mind goal was to not just survive but thrive in my family's circumstances and the years to come. I felt like I was the hobbit, Bilbo Baggins, going on an adventure to see how the pain and discomfort I was about to endure for many ceaseless months would be minimal compared to the plentiful benefits and joyful opportunities that would be awaiting my family and me in our bright future.

* * *

When you embody resiliency, you learn how to effectively and positively react, respond, and recover from your life-threatening challenges. Sometimes, it is hard to imagine we're capable of overcoming our life-altering circumstances. Resilience requires ongoing practice and reinforcement; like muscles in the body, we all have them, but developing stronger muscles involves using more energy, practicing regularly, recovering, and challenging yourself.

Lacrosse granted me numerous opportunities to practice and reinforce resiliency that I could apply to my family's circumstances and beyond. The importance of resiliency was especially prevalent on April 24, 2012, when my team played our rivals, the Panthers. My mom planned on attending the game; however, she told me earlier that afternoon she had a meeting at the hospital to discuss my dad's upcoming radiation treatments that were supposed to start the following week. When I made my way back to the sideline after the coin toss in the captain's circle, I saw my mom wave at me over by the metal chain-link fence.

"Hi, what's up?" I asked her. "The game's going to start."

"I know. Did you put sunscreen on?"

"Yes, mom." I mumbled.

"Good," she hesitated. "Listen, I got back from the appointment with the radiation doctor."

Daunting thoughts and questions filled my brain.

"Yeah, how did it go?" I asked.

"Well, your dad is going to be treated every other day for the next few months. They also told us that . . .." My mom was holding back the truth, afraid of sharing the news.

"The doctors said what?" I asked my mom, nudging her to finish her sentence.

In a calm, yet terrified voice, she replied: "Your dad will lose his entire sense of smell and some of his ability to generate saliva."

I was frozen. It was a good thing no one could hear my mind because it was screaming, brewing a headache. The referee's whistle broke up my thoughts and emotions—it was game time, but I was in distress. I looked to mom's expression and body language for an explanation but found nothing.

"I can't do this . . .." The panic was rising in my throat.

"I'm sorry about this, sweet pea. You had to know . . .," my mom replied. I did not answer her because I was already walking onto the field toward the draw circle.

As I pulled my goggles down and bit down on my mouth guard, I approached the center of the turf field where the referee and a player from the opposing team wearing jersey number ten were waiting. The referee placed the ball in between the two pockets of our lacrosse sticks and backed away to blow the whistle and begin the game.

Lifting my stick over my head, I jumped up to retrieve the ball free falling above our heads. The second the ball was cradled in the pocket of my lacrosse stick I immediately clutched my stick tightly, brought it close to my chest and sprinted away toward our offense.

I ran past the forty-yard line . . . the thirty . . . just barely reaching the twenty-five when number ten forcefully checked me from behind. I was flung forward, face first into the turf and the ball rolled out of the head of my stick. By the time I was able to push myself off the ground and retrieve my stick, an opposing defensive player ran the ball down the other way and scored a through-the-legs shot against our goalie.

I jogged back over to the center, shaking it off. The referee got the draw ready and blew the whistle. Again, I jumped immediately, getting nice height, but number ten shoved the butt-end of her stick into my chest. She retrieved the ball before me and headed down the field toward her offense.

The draws continued and the defeat progressed, creating a cyclical pattern. Number ten targeted me, and her other teammates followed her lead. Even when I did not have the ball in my possession, I was tripped, slashed, stepped on, and shoved.

I couldn't do anything: throw, catch, run, shoot, or breathe. It was like I forgot how to play. My team relied on me as one of our best players and I was getting crushed in front of them, falling victim. I felt the distress of my dad's cancer take over me; the thought of the pain and suffering my dad would go through and not knowing how things would turn out for my family plagued my mind.

The strength I had mustered upon hearing the announcement of my dad's diagnosis, during the surgery day, and throughout the prolonged weeks witnessing my dad in pain vanished into thin air. Despite the physical removal of his cancer, I feared it would continue to harm my dad and continue to haunt my family for ages.

I felt all my strength and determination crumble to dust and started to sob. Despite it all, I continued to play while choking on my tears.

* * *

I eventually made it over to the team bench at the end of the first half. I kept my head low to avoid the worried glances from my teammates and surveyed the damage: bruises swelled on my skin, turf beads covered my legs and fell into my shoes, and the afternoon sun made the open, bloody cuts on my cheek and arms burn. A moment later, my coach, Mrs.

Hartman, took a seat to my right on the bench, wrapping her arm around my shoulders.

"Nicole," she took a breath before continuing, "Don't let this beat you. You're too good of a player to let the other team and the cancer control you."

I turned to look her as she continued to speak, my face covered in dried tears, melted sunscreen, and cuts.

"You can do this. We need our best player. The strength you need is already within you to become stronger and better than ever before." Right as I was about to reply, the start of the second half was announced.

I walked back onto the field again as the encouraging words of Coach Hartman rang in my mind, channeling a new calm and driven energy. I felt like a water cooler of ice was dumped on me, waking up to realize I was not ever going to let fear or intimidation get the best of me again.

During the second half, I maintained my composure, upheld my strength, and kept both feet on the ground at all times. I won every draw against number ten, getting her as flustered and frustrated as I was earlier. I outran and outplayed our rivals, racking up goals and assists and completing new tricks and moves I never tried before.

I felt unstoppable!

The cheers from my team, coaches, and the sidelines were impenetrable, keeping my spirits up and my adrenaline pumping. I had the resiliency, energy, and determination to play as hard as I could and enjoyed all the thrills of lacrosse as the rival team's coach screamed to her players: "Stop that girl! Stop number twenty! She's outplaying us!"

TWEET! TWEET! TWEET!

The whistle echoed in the stadium, ending the game and crowning my team victorious. Several of my teammates on and off the field ran over to embrace me and celebrate one of the greatest comebacks we had ever witnessed.

* * *

The real victory of that game was knowing that Mrs. Hartmann was right: I realized what I am truly capable of if I believe I can do it. I had all the strength I needed within me to persevere and have confidence in my abilities. I regained control of the situation, my thoughts, and emotions to come back as a better version of myself.

Learning the lesson of resiliency from my lacrosse game created a mental reservoir of perseverance for me, granting me the ability to draw upon my strength when I needed to overcome adversities.

Resiliency gave me the strength to cope with, grow, and heal from my family's derailment. I utilized my resiliency to work through my dad's radiation treatments, to put forth my best effort into my academics, to have the courage to share my book I wrote with my dad, and to see this sudden life plot twist through until the very end.

After that game and throughout my dad's cancer journey, resilience taught me that I'm not defined by what my family and I went through, but by how I chose to live my life from that moment onward—I decided my attitude, mindset, thoughts, behaviors, and perspectives. What I place my focus and energy on is what will manifest. I chose to finish that lacrosse game, to sit through my dad's twelve-hour surgery, to embrace all the good our family's setback would bring us, and to discover what the next chapter of my life had waiting for me.

Resiliency is an essential component of overcoming difficult challenges or obstacles that arise throughout life; no matter how many times we fall down, we must get right back up again.

CHAPTER 8

COMPASSION

"We all must make it a priority to acknowledge and appreciate all the people who are important to you, especially the partners who gave you encouragement and expressed genuine interest in your ongoing recovery." [29]

—JIM UHRIG, AUTHOR, *PARTNERS 4 LIFE*

During Angela's early adolescent years, not only was she diagnosed with major depressive disorder and a generalized anxiety disorder, but her brother was diagnosed with Asperger's and suffered from depression. Battling her mental health issues through therapy and medications while helping her brother was far from easy.

Angela carried significant burdens at an early age, yet the event that took an immense toll on Angela's recovery from depression was the loss of her father to alcoholism when she

29 Jim Uhrig, *Partners 4 Life: The Importance of Partners in Surviving an Organ Transplant* (Bloomington: iUniverse, 2014), 91.

was seventeen. Her parents divorced when she was six years old, and Angela was nine the last time she saw her father before he was laying in his casket at his funeral.

For many months preceding her father's funeral, Angela experienced endless anxiety attacks that varied in severity and frequency; she was plagued by memories from when she was very young and witnessed her father become extremely inebriated several times a week. Upon attending a four-year university, Angela received support from the counseling center, her family, and closest friends to work through her anxiety and depression. She gained assurance that there's a light at the end of the tunnel after going through unfortunate times.

"Even through some of my worst days, I've learned to appreciate the fact that without the terribly bad days, there would be no true meaning for a really good day," Angela stated.

In addition to prioritizing her mental health, Angela became an emergency medical technician (EMT) and hopes to become a surgical oncologist or a physician's assistant. The biggest aspiration Angela shared with me that she learned from her own struggles is that she strives to prevent and ease the pain of others as much as she can. She believes kindness and happiness are often the best medicine for overcoming all obstacles in life. Additionally, Angela recognizes that demonstrating compassion is a necessity in her profession.

"It is important to be kind to others no matter what because you never know what someone might be going through,"

Angela emphasized. "I want to take this into my career and treat each patient I'll encounter with nothing but kindness because the compassion I have received gives me strength every single day to continually combat my mental health."

Early in her collegiate experience, Angela was selected to be a Peer Health Advocate at her university. A Peer Health Advocate is a community outreach position that allowed her to connect with peers on campus and creatively educate them on various health-related topics. This position enabled Angela to be compassionate toward others by elaborating on her personal hardships and actively assisting those in her life struggling with mental health issues.

"Being a Peer Health Advocate," Angela explained, "has allowed me to grow from my experiences and encourage growth in others that may be experiencing the same things I have dealt with." This position, in addition to her EMT duties, has further emphasized the importance of being compassionate throughout all walks of life.

Angela has revamped the definition of compassion to extend beyond simple acts of kindness; embodying compassion allows you to notice the pain of others beyond one's own suffering and to do the best you can to alleviate the pain of others. In addition, Angela learned how going the extra mile to be compassionate has served her well in personal life and will continue to do so in her profession. Compassion softens you as a person, if you let it, and allows you to be sympathetic toward others and recognize their pain.

* * *

According to leading meditation teacher Christina Feldman and psychologist Willem Kuyken in their published journal *Contemporary Buddhism*, compassion is having the aspiration to heal and grow upon opening up to the reality of suffering. When you can imagine the suffering of those around you and have a reference point in your own life for the amount of distress someone might be going through, it better equips you to give them grace and assist them through the tough times. [30]

Showing compassion means putting yourself in someone else's shoes to devote both your time and thoughts into understanding someone else's situation. Compassion requires patience and active listening abilities to navigate through sensitive conversations to enable you to actively assist someone to take action to improve their lives.

I received absolutely no shortage of compassion when my dad was diagnosed with cancer. Beating cancer was a team effort. People were always in our corner encouraging us like a personal cheering squad. Through my family's circumstances, I learned that friendships and partnerships should never be taken for granted. Hard times won't last forever, but true friendships do. Friends will never leave your side and always have your back through thick and thin.

When my dad endured his battle with cancer, not only did my friendships and family relationships strengthen, but new acquaintances emerged in the most unlikely yet meaningful

---

30 Christina Feldman and Willem Kuyken, "Compassion in the Landscape of Suffering," *Contemporary Buddism - An Interdisciplinary Journal* 1, no. 12 (2011): 143–155.

ways. They discerned my emotions and gave me the exact help I felt I needed without having to ask for it. They took away some of my suffering, walked a mile in my shoes, and deeply cared about my happiness.

Most importantly, these individuals demonstrated genuine kindness toward me, teaching me what it means to be compassionate.

Although my support system may not have gone through the same challenges that I did, their compassion still made all the difference in the world to me. It helped me tap into my own power of compassion and courage to persevere through my dad's life-threatening diagnosis. Through the next few pages, I would like to shine a spotlight on two unsung supporters who demonstrated genuine compassion toward me.

* * *

The first illustration of how the simplest acts of kindness touched my heart occurred the morning after my dad's surgery on February 11, 2012. I woke promptly at 6:15 a.m. without any alarms that morning. I got out of bed, put on my slippers, and threw on one of my lacrosse sweatshirts for an extra layer of warmth. I quietly headed down the hallway toward the steps, making sure I didn't step on any of the squeaky spots on the wood floor to avoid waking my mom.

When I got downstairs, I noticed a bright and blinding white light coming in through the windows from outside. I walked over to the front door to take a glimpse outside only to find a fresh, three-inch blanket of snow and some flakes still fluttering down from above. What caught me off guard was seeing our neighbor across the street, Mr. Winslow, start to shovel our driveway.

Wishing to help my neighbor with what used to be my dad's chore but was now added to my laundry list, I shuffled over to the hall closet to retrieve my puffy coat, a pair of gloves, a little gray cap, and my father's heavy winter boots. Haphazardly tucking my pajama bottoms into the boots, I unlocked the front door and cautiously headed down the stone pathway to my driveway.

"Good morning, Mr. Winslow!" I called out to him.

He turned around to greet me. "Good morning, Nicole. It's nice to see you."

"It is a bit early to be shoveling," I muttered as I waddled through the snow. "I didn't know it was going to snow this much overnight."

"Well, that's winter in Pittsburgh, as per usual," Mr. Winslow chuckled as he pushed the snow into a pile along the sides of my driveway.

I still couldn't comprehend why Mr. Winslow was out here on a Saturday morning shoveling snow from our driveway. I could clearly see from where I was standing that he hadn't shoveled his own driveway yet.

"You know, you don't have to do this. I can handle it myself. I've helped my dad loads of times before . . ." I honestly admitted.

Mr. Winslow paused a moment from shoveling and turned to face me.

"You and your family shouldn't have to worry, Nicole," he reassuringly said. He paused, a smile forming on his face. "The very least I can do is shovel your driveway."

I did not know what to say. This small yet touching favor that my neighbor was doing for my family without hesitation warmed my heart, healing the bruises the last several weeks of pain and distress left on my body and soul. It is amazing how much people are willing to go out of their way to take time to help others. The act of kindness of shoveling my family's driveway created an endless wave of happiness and comfort within me; years later, my heart still fills with joy every time I think about this moment. Mr. Winslow's compassion taught me that an act of kindness does not need to be a grand gesture—a simple action or thought can go the distance.

"Thank you, sir!" I genuinely replied.

"Of course, Nicole." Mr. Winslow resumed shoveling as I bounded back up the walkway to the front door, reminding myself that I could not delay getting back to the hospital that morning to see my dad any longer.

* * *

Compassion brings out the best in all of us. If we are actively demonstrating compassion and are invested in making others happy, there are no boundaries to the amount of love, peace, and happiness we can bring into the lives of others and ourselves. No matter how small the act of kindness may be, there is always an opportunity to make a change in other people's lives.

The other uncredited helper exemplified a deeper meaning of compassion beyond simple acts of kindness—"to suffer with"—which requires a deep, emotional awareness of the suffering of another coupled with the wish to relieve the pain or distress being endured.

One evening in March, after attending a lacrosse practice, wading through a swamp of homework and reading material, and spending a majority of the night helping my mom take care of my dad who was in pain, I failed to finish the assigned reading of *Ethan Frome* for my Honors English class.

The next day in eighth period, my English professor, Mrs. Lattimore, decided to hand out a pop quiz worth twenty points on the assigned reading that I did not finish. I stared at the four short-answer questions that required explanations, examples, and details—none of which I could provide. I felt nervous, scared, and on the brink of tears. I got out of my seat, as if someone cast a spell over me, and walked right past Mrs. Lattimore's desk and out into the hallway.

I leaned my back against the row of red lockers a few feet from the classroom door. Mrs. Lattimore hurriedly walked out of her classroom to find me.

"Is everything alright, Nicole?" She said in a low, but startled voice that was out of earshot of the other students in the classroom.

"I . . . no . . ." I admitted. I went about briefly explaining how awful it's been to put the effort into my schoolwork and allocating the time to complete it. This was the first and only time in my entire academic career that I failed to fully finish a homework assignment or a test.

Mrs. Lattimore listened to me intently. When I finished explaining the events of the prior evening (and month), she embraced me warmly.

"When we started to read *Ethan Frome*, I had a gut feeling that it was going to be sensitive for you to read. I should not have put you through the struggles of reading that book. You may be excused from all assignments related to the book. I'm sorry . . .."

One of my teachers was sorry for me. That had never happened. Mrs. Lattimore was genuinely concerned about how my family's traumatic derailment was disrupting my ability to focus on my schoolwork. She could visualize how the grim themes of *Ethan Frome* could have been interfering with my mental and emotional well-being and became aware of my personal struggles. The responses and actions she took to alleviate my stress for the foreseeable future were sincerely enlightening.

Also, I learned that compassion significantly improved my relationships with others. It was a relief to know that at least one of my teachers, Mrs. Lattimore, comprehended some of the distress I was continually enduring on the home front. Furthermore, being fully present and simply listening can be one of the most compassionate acts you can offer to someone. It was one of the authentic ways my teacher demonstrated compassion toward me as she comprehended the difficulty I had in simply reading a page of *Ethan Frome* or any reading assignment.

As I was about to reply back to her, Mrs. Lattimore went into the classroom, returning momentarily with my books and tote.

"Why don't you go sit in the library for the rest of the period? I think getting space away from the classroom will do you some good."

I nodded my head. She smiled slightly, "And don't fret about any homework for now, wait until after we finish reading *Ethan Frome.*"

I acknowledged her statement with a smile and several nods of my head as I walked down the hall toward the library. I spent the remainder of the school day sitting in one of the faded beanbag chairs in the fiction section of the library, silently praying I would never walk out of an exam or class like that ever again.

* * *

The compassion Mr. Winslow and Mrs. Lattimore expressed to me proved that compassion is contagious and helped me become more compassionate. This form of heart-felt support inspired me to incorporate compassion as a routine during my dad's recovery. Compassion allowed me to better access and meet my dad's ongoing needs to relieve any pain, distress, or hardship that was at the root of his suffering.

In the first weeks after returning home from the hospital, my dad had trouble eating solid food; all he could eat for about a month was mashed potatoes and chicken broth. I found this odd at first but seeing him struggle in pain as he swallowed a spoonful of yogurt showed me just how hard it was for him to eat. Watching my dad be uncomfortable taking a nap in a reclining chair, watching a sporting event on television, or trying to pay attention to a conversation we were having was dreadful. I did not have the power to entirely rid my dad of his pain; however, I knew I had capacity to be compassionate.

I became present and patient with my dad during his recovery to relieve just a little of his distress. On several occasions, I retrieved my dad's Bible upstairs when he didn't have the endurance to climb up the stairs, prepared a meal for him that he could digest, or joined him outside on the back patio as we sat in silence, taking in the fresh air in our fenced-in backyard. These simple acts of kindness reaffirmed my unconditional love and acceptance for my dad and left a soft smile forming on my dad's face, an appreciative "thank you" escaping from chapped lips.

> When something tragic happens, it pulls people together to create a strong foundation of compassion and support.

It is a rewarding and fulfilling feeling to know I helped my dad overcome his cancer and the other struggles he experienced post-surgery. Approaching others who are experiencing difficult times as if their struggles were my own allowed me to see the true value of others and the potential good in everyone.

Each person will fight a difficult battle; however, the ways in which we touch other people's lives by exercising compassion will never fade away.

CHAPTER 9

ADAPTABILITY

"When we're no longer able to change a situation, we're challenged to change ourselves." [31]

—VIKTOR FRANKL

Marissa grew up in a military family, an unusual life circumstance that less than 1 percent of American kids experience in their lifetime. Constant change monopolized Marissa's life: she had lived in six states and on numerous occasions her dad was deployed anywhere from six months to a year, leaving all those responsibilities behind while her mom worked full-time. Every time her dad returned, he had to be reintroduced into her life. Furthermore, since her dad was a military officer with tremendous leadership qualities and over twenty-five years of service, Marissa grew up having to meet high expectations and acquired a competitive drive.

31 Viktor E. Frankl, *Man's Search for Meaning* (Boston: Beacon Press, 2006), 17-154.

Every two or three years when her family had to move near a different military base, Marissa's life changed, requiring her to continually reestablish herself. Despite the struggles of finding a sense of normalcy in her life and a steady group of friends growing up, Marissa revealed one of the biggest strengths of being a military kid that shaped her personality, attitude, and beliefs.

"Having to reestablish myself all the time because my life was always uprooted and moved," Marissa explained, "required adaptability. I think this played a significant role in who I am now and how I traversed numerous obstacles."

When Marissa went to college, she realized her four-year institution would be the place where she had lived the longest. She never felt homesick, though. Adaptability continued to serve Marissa well, not only in embracing uncertainty, but learning to go with the flow and realizing everything ends up working out. Marissa experienced some discouraging setbacks early in her collegiate years, such as being turned down for several leadership opportunities and internship programs that she was one of few finalists for.

Yet, Marissa discovered how growing up in a military family, and the experiences that came with it that led her to be adaptable, applied to her college setbacks; rather than turning away from them, Marissa embraced adaptability to set her up for success and immense joy in the long run.

One of the many opportunities Marissa recently immersed herself in is a campaign with the Leukemia and Lymphoma Society of Northern Ohio (LLS). She and her team were able to raise $31,399 to support families with children battling cancer. Also, she was named the LLS of Northern Ohio's Woman of the Year! After an incredibly successful fundraiser, Marissa aspires to achieve a balance between her two passions: pursuing a career in human resources and giving back through nonprofit work.

"If I didn't learn how to handle uncertainty and rejection to see what great opportunities were awaiting me, I wouldn't have found the LLS organization," Marissa shared. "I'm lucky to have found these opportunities that have guided me to my purpose: serving others."

With a strong stability in faith and perseverance in uncertain times, Marissa believes everything that is meant to be, will be. Even though we may not have control over what happens in our lives, we must believe great things are yet to come on our life's journey.

"I have definitely experienced quite a few obstacles," Marissa said. "However, embracing adaptability helped me to see that there's always something so much bigger and more meaningful waiting for me. It takes only one 'yes,' one positive indication, or one small win to make the journey and struggles worthwhile."

* * *

Marissa's story exemplifies why it is so critical to learn how to adapt during life's disruptive conditions rather than to sink to rock bottom. Adaptability is the ability to quickly respond to changes in your external environment. It is a fundamental asset to possess because change in life is inevitable. This ability to adjust to new conditions while still aiming for your purpose in life becomes a piece of the larger puzzle of overcoming your personal life's setbacks. According to the management consulting company, Robert Half International, adaptability allows us to reevaluate our current situation, learn from the unexpected changes, and adjust our actions, attitude, behavior, or approach to doing things to suit our new circumstances without any major setbacks.[32]

Adaptability becomes a necessity when you have to adjust to changes you have no control over; it enables you to look for new ways to handle multiple tasks and work under time or other constraints. It can be utilized when you have to think creatively to either learn new techniques or explore various avenues as a way of embracing change. Regardless of what types of derailments or changes with which you are dealing, adaptability helps you refrain from getting flustered or panicked when things do not go according to plan. If you become adaptable, you are more likely to handle change with ease and smoothness.

Flexibility is a key component of adaptability—it is about getting comfortable with being uncomfortable, becoming resourceful, being receptive to new ideas, and maximizing your functionality in the face of distress. Having contingency plans and learning how to respond optimistically to change will help you handle transitions and be flexible in the ever-changing world surrounding you.

32 "Adaptability Skills," Robert Half, accessed August 24, 2020.

My dad's cancer diagnosis was a startling wake-up call after experiencing fifteen years of consistent patterns, normalcy, and routines. I always knew, deep down, that unforeseeable change would eventually run its course in my life, but not in the extreme way of threatening my dad's life. During the many months after my dad's diagnosis, change hovered over me like an ominous cloud ready to either pour buckets of water or part to reveal the radiant sun's rays.

Since the day I learned about my family's life-changing situation, I quickly discovered there is no true, concrete definition for normal. Establishing a sense of normalcy is dependent upon your current circumstances and is completely subjective because we filter the world through our own lenses and belief systems. When my family's life was turned upside down and inside out, I quickly learned I couldn't go back to the normalcy of the life in which I was fortunate enough to have grown up.

Adaptability gave me the confidence to navigate the temporary, unfortunate circumstances that swept into my family's life; being adaptable and flexible allowed me to accept whatever is happening is what it is, even if it wasn't what I wanted or expected. I holistically accepted the present moment as it was and decided to work through each moment as it came. Throughout my dad's obstacle, I continually strove to instill and reinforce the ideals of being adaptable and flexible.

With adaptability, I have found that the next door or pathway opens when one door closes.

In addition to being flexible, impermanence is another facet of adaptability that plays a significant role when navigating traumatic circumstances. Impermanence is about realizing nothing lasts forever and will eventually pass; you become free from your attachments and ease into a new sense of normalcy. Impermanence coincides with adaptability and flexibility, allowing you to take things moment-by-moment amid change and pain.

You should not feel rigid, angry, or stuck in your old ways, mindset, or routines; you need to learn to go with the flow, let things go, and allow things to just be. Rather than trying to force everything to be black and white, adaptability, flexibility, and impermanence make the gray area the new norm. It will push you out of your comfort zone, increase your chances of succeeding, and help you seize all the new experiences life will bring.

My family learned to cope with the uncertainties that revolved around my dad's extremely rare cancer. The trailblazing medical professionals walked alongside my family into a thick fog of unknowns. No one knew back then what caused this cancer to develop, what the post-surgery recovery would be like, what side effects my dad would experience, or how much time my dad had left before the cancer took over.

"Exactly, how long will the procedure take?"

"Will he require chemotherapy and radiation treatments?"

"Why can't he sit in the sun or lay flat on his back?"

These questions and more echoed in our house, the hospital, and doctors' offices. We were absolutely terrified by having no obvious, easy, or straightforward answers to our questions. However, what propelled my family and medical professionals to persevere and navigate through the dense fog was realizing the battle with this cancer was not going to happen all at once. We would need to take one step, one breath, and one moment at a time.

* * *

Throughout the duration of my dad's cancer journey, we had our fair share of ups and downs. Some days were better than others; my dad would make remarkable progress one day but would backtrack a few steps the next. There were days when my dad looked lively, got a good report after completing a treatment, and felt his pain diminish, which gave me hope and reassurance that we were making forward progress.

Then suddenly, we would backtrack; my dad wouldn't keep his medicine down, stayed up all night dealing with excruciating pain, and felt helpless like all the progress we made previously was for nothing. My family and I learned to not only adjust to the new changes that sprung into our lives but to hold tightly to our faith to believe we could navigate through these changes and adapt to keep moving forward.

When abrupt change interrupted my family's life, some initial adjustments needed to be established: my family postponed or rescheduled events we had planned in advance such as a spring break mini getaway, visiting relatives, or going to the mall for an afternoon. We couldn't go visit Corey at his university, my parents couldn't attend a majority of my lacrosse games or tournaments, and we readjusted all our schedules to make sure my dad made all his necessary appointments and treatments.

Originally, I got flustered and annoyed that we were not able to do our usual activities as a family. Yet, the importance of adaptability, flexibility, and impermanence became prevalent when I devoted time to discern these were transitory adjustments. In time, my family and I would be able to go back to spending quality family time, explore places across the country, and attend fun events.

Nothing ended or got canceled. We just postponed it or put it on hold until we hurdled our current life obstacle.

I found closure in knowing nothing is permanent—even my family's life-altering setback.

The adjustments were necessary for the time being, and by adapting and working through these challenging times, we found the light that emerged from the unknown darkness.

This moment-by-moment mindset became prevalent in distinctly personal ways in my life. With my family and home life in shambles and complications at every turn, my academics, extra-curricular activities, and social life were no exceptions to the disarray. The endless adjustments I had to make in my life amid my family's traumatic circumstances required me to wear many hats. In a single day, I had five primary roles: daughter, caregiver, student, friend, and teammate.

Certain roles proved to be more burdensome some days than others. I had difficulty constantly staying afloat when the adversities in life tried to bring me down. Balancing these roles equally proved incredibly stressful and confusing; my frustration provoked thoughts of waiting to give up and drop everything.

I would often find myself thinking on repeat,

"What should I prioritize first: attending an extra lacrosse practice before the next game against our biggest rival or finishing an essay for my history class?"

"How can I help my mom with chores around the house while she is preoccupied with taking care of my dad?"

"Why have I been assigned all these roles? How will I possibly manage them all and achieve positive results?"

These daily questions I asked myself had no clear black or white answers. Yet, by navigating through these roles and difficulties they brought, I knew everything would be temporary, blowing past me like a gust of wind.

With my only fixed routine being my class and lacrosse schedules, I learned things have a way of working out, even if they do not go the way I initially planned them to. Despite how uncertain my life was with abrupt changes erupting out of the blue, I always knew I would get my homework done, study for a test, and be able to attend lacrosse practice on time. I broke down each moment in my life like my lacrosse playback: each move or action was a step in the right direction that allowed me to confront the adversity in my life in strides.

Being flexible and recognizing the impermanence of the challenge allowed me to become an agent of change during my family's situation. I dealt with any impeding setback not only quickly but also seamlessly and positively. Being adaptable helped me maintain a calm and optimistic composure whenever things started to go downhill. Over time, I found that embracing adaptability leveraged new capabilities for me. It taught me that I can't drown myself with thoughts of what could have been or burden myself with checking off every single item on a monstrous size to-do list; rather, I need to adjust my thoughts to focus on what I can do in this moment.

Moments were all my family and I had. They are all any of us have.

You are supposed to enjoy and cherish life through moments. Any moment in our life can become full of changes, uncertainties, and transitions that we can welcome, try to ignore, or fight against. These changes can be exciting, challenging, sometimes sad or scary, and even frustrating. The life changes we accept and embrace are the ones we can grow from, becoming stronger and more resilient because of them.

The ability to adapt is a valuable skill that will better enable you to handle various life stages, challenges, and transitions. Adaptability provides us with the strength to recover and rebound from our hardships so we can succeed and seize the bountiful opportunities awaiting us beyond these moments.

CHAPTER 10

GRATITUDE

"The next time you're faced with something that's unexpected, unwanted, and uncertain, consider that it just may be a gift."[33]

—STACEY KRAMER

On January 15, 2020, a premature diagnosis of temporomandibular joint (TMJ) pain inflicting the left side of Christian's face evolved into spindle cell or sclerosing rhabdomyosarcoma, an incredibly rare cancer of the jawbone. Barely two weeks after the tumor was detected, surgeons successfully removed the tumor that was classified as a stage 3B cancer. They removed the back half of his jawbone and replaced it with the bone from his fibula and a 3-D titanium plate. Due to the sensitivity of the facial nerves disrupted during the surgery, the left side of Christian's face became temporarily paralyzed; doctors expect him to recover and regain mobility with time.

33 *TED*, "Stacey Kramer: The Best Gift I Ever Survived," October 8, 2010, video, 6:26.

With the assistance of a temporary feeding tube and tracheostomy—a small cylinder inside the windpipe that helps someone breathe—Christian was hospitalized for over two weeks after the surgery. To reduce the chances of tumor recurrence, in late February, Christian embarked on his yearlong chemotherapy journey. His thirty-three proton beam radiation therapy treatments began at the end of March. Despite the overwhelming odyssey of appointments and treatments ahead, Christian discovered how his diagnosis was more of a blessing than a burden.

"This diagnosis made me realize just how important gratitude is and how every moment and every interaction is an opportunity to give thanks to God and occurs by the grace of God," Christian shared. "Even the cancer is something to thank God for because it's a drastic, yet humbling wake-up call to take stock of how I'd been living and what needs to change."

Throughout his diagnosis and recovery, Christian has found marvelous ways to rethink his current circumstances as a transformative process. Christian has found strength in God's Word, humility, gratitude, and the power of prayer along with the support and words of encouragement from his family and friends.

"I was one of those people who prayed half-heartedly before this experience like 'God, I hope you can do something for me, but I'm not sure if it's going to work,'" Christian explained to me. "But thanks be to God, I've really seen prayer work in the midst of my circumstances."

One of the countless examples of how the power of prayer and miracles manifested for Christian came a week after his surgery. For unknown reasons, he developed an infection that gave him a high fever and caused his heart to race uncontrollably. Terrified he might be taken back to the operating room, Christian, his wife, and brother asked for the intercessions of the Virgin Mary; they prayed for roughly an hour while the infectious workup began. Christian's fever then broke before any new antibiotics were administered or any tests came back.

In only the first few months of his one-year recovery, Christian has unlocked immense strength and perseverance by finding ways to be grateful every day. He believes manifesting gratitude through thankfulness allowed for miracles to occur every day and found praying is one of the many intentional ways to express and demonstrate gratitude.

"This experience has made me want to become a 'prayer warrior,' not only for myself but for other people. We commonly say we pray with gratitude because it's the least we can do, but it's actually the most and the best we can do for ourselves and others!"

* * *

Taking a moment to give thanks and be grateful in times of uncertainty can transform your life beyond your current circumstances like it has for Christian. Gratitude has the power to heal, cultivate healthy relationships, bring hope, and help us cope with difficult times; it's a central component and practice of spirituality that can strengthen one's faith in a multitude of ways.

Being grateful transports you into a new state of mindfulness and awareness. It sharpens your powers of observation to discover all the interlinking layers of life, to cherish all the little pleasures, and to acquire a deep, steadfast affirmation that goodness exists. Additionally, gratitude helps us to contemplate our place in the intricate, interdependent network of life—an inherent realization that sparks joy and appreciation.

Robert Emmons, the world's leading gratitude expert, psychology professor at the University of California-Davis, and founding editor-in-chief of *The Journal of Positive Psychology*, argues that being grateful requires two components:

1. Recognizing there are good things or positive outcomes in the world like benefits and gifts
2. Discovering the primary sources for these positive outcomes are often outside of ourselves

Both components are brought upon us by external sources such as other people or even higher powers. Emmons' two-step process affirms that good things in your life come from outside of yourself during the ups and downs of life. Categorized as an intense feeling and incredible state of being, gratitude is strongly and consistently associated with greater happiness, stronger faith, mental health improvements, and better life satisfaction.[34]

I recognize I had numerous positives for which to be grateful in 2012. We were fortunate the medical professionals had

---

34 *Greater Good Science Center*, "Robert Emmons: Benefits of Gratitude," November 19, 2010, video, 10:35.

suspicions early on—a gut feeling they should complete more tests to find an explanation for my dad's difficulty breathing. The doctors not only had intuition about the cancerous tumor early on, but they also worked effortlessly and miraculously to keep my dad alive. My family managed to go the distance and prevail in our distressing setback despite not having any definite answers or concrete explanations regarding the surgery and its long-term effects. Everything fell into place and proved better than we expected because none of our worst-case scenarios became a reality.

I wholeheartedly believe God has amazing things in store for me that I can't even begin to contemplate or imagine. During my family's life-altering circumstances and beyond, my trust in God grew stronger. I accepted my circumstances and began viewing my temporary setbacks as teaching moments.

Through these teaching moments, I began to witness my beyond on the horizon—I discovered I had a bright future ahead of me; I envisioned myself attending a university I could call home, building long-lasting friendships, diving into opportunities related to my passions, and finding dream opportunities in human resources. Most importantly, I saw greater and better things ahead for me and my family in the foreseeable future. Tapping into gratitude allowed me to trust the path that has been uniquely designed for me, be still in the present, and acknowledge I have a purpose and reason to be here.

* * *

Reflecting on my family's derailment with cancer, I think my dad became a miracle and a living angel on earth. Although my dad endured extreme physical and psychological distress, he never gave up hope. After each appointment, phone call, and treatment, he graciously thanked each medical personnel who made sure he had the best possible care. Most importantly, my dad was thankful for me, my mom, and Corey for providing unconditional love, having the determination to thrive through our setback, and becoming a stronger and happier family.

My dad always knew deep down that things were going to be okay and we were going to get through it together. He believed God was watching over us, guiding us on the path to recovery and salvation. If my dad wasn't sleeping, eating, or attending his appointments, he was reading scripture, silently praying with his head bowed and eyes closed, asking for forgiveness and guidance, or tightly clasping his gold cross that he kept with him at all times.

At least once a day—usually at the first sign of daylight or in the stillness of the night—I would find my dad either silently reading prayers to himself or writing scripture from the Bible. As I observed my dad from afar, I felt inner peace and tranquility that wrapped our family and house in a warm embrace, protecting us from fear, toxic thoughts, negativity, and doubt. Even as he sat quietly during these intentional, grateful moments in the reclining chair next to the floor lamp, the light and peace my dad experienced illuminated the entire house brilliantly.

In moments like these I overflowed with gratitude—for my dad's life, for the doctor's quick intervention, and for the opportunity to come closer together as a family. Gratitude refocused my attention on what my family and I *had* instead of what we *lacked*, reminding me we should never take anything for granted. By refocusing my attention on my family's blessings, I have become grateful for the precious moments and quality time I have with my family.

* * *

Gratitude is a choice. We choose between fear or faith—despair or hope. We all have something to be grateful for and there is no limit on gratitude. By embracing and practicing gratitude in your everyday life, blessings and miracles will start flooding in.

One of the blessings I received happened on the very same day I found out about my dad's diagnosis. After the longest hour of my life spent attempting to digest the shocking news, I retreated to my bedroom. I shut the door behind me and cried, slowly sinking to the floor.

Several moments later, I unconsciously grabbed my purple Motorola phone from my bed and called my best friend, Mackenzie, who lived two minutes down the road from me. Mackenzie had a strong, faithful foundation since her father was a senior pastor at one of the local churches in my community. She was the first person I called because at that moment—crying as I sat on the uncomfortable, cold floor of my room—I not only needed one of my best friends, but I also yearned for a glimpse of hope and faithful reassurance that I could persevere through this uncertainty and stay strong for my family.

It rang two times before I heard her voice on the other line.

"Hey, how are you?" she answered.

"I need to tell you something." I was still sobbing slightly so when I talked, it was noticeable I was in the middle of a breakdown.

"What's wrong? Is everything alright?" Mackenzie sounded distraught.

In about a minute, I summarized the conversation I had with my parents earlier about my dad's cancer diagnosis and his upcoming surgery.

"Nicole . . . I'm so sorry." From over the phone, it sounded like Mackenzie was holding back tears too.

"I don't know what to do," I continued to sob.

"It's going to be okay . . . I'm here for you and I'm going to pray for you and your family every day."

"Thank you . . ." was all I could manage to say. "I'll talk to you later."

"Okay. If not, I'll see you in school."

I hung up the phone and remained on my hardwood floor until the sound of my phone vibrating on a loose floorboard broke the silence. I retrieved my phone to find a text message awaiting me. It was a message with the inspiring words of God from Mackenzie.

> “I can do all things through him who gives me strength.”
>
> —PHILIPPIANS 4:13.[35]

Upon reading the line of scripture several times in the stillness of my bedroom, I scrambled over to my desk. I wrote the sentence down and taped it on the mirror over my dresser. It would serve as my reminder each morning and night that I was going to get through these hard times and we were going to be okay.

This line from Philippians struck a new chord within me; I found this greater connection to God, my faith, and my purpose.

I was grateful for such a good friend who could help guide me spiritually and for feeling God’s peace, love, and hope within me through the bible passage. Gratitude washed over my soul every single time I read that sentence, reminding me that by focusing on what I could do each moment, my infinite bounty of goodness and positivity would flourish with God by my side.

* * *

Another remarkable discovery I made during my family’s distressing situation was I didn’t have to look far to discover several amazing people were walking alongside me

---

35 Phi. 4:13 (NT).

throughout the entire journey; they worked in the smallest, yet most meaningful ways in my life. I can't express enough gratitude toward these incredible individuals; they were one of the many motivational reasons why I knew my family and I would prevail under my dad's life-threatening situation.

First, I'm grateful for Mrs. Irene, one of my high school teachers. She had always been one of my biggest cheerleaders during my high school career, so I told her about my dad's diagnosis before any other teacher. Mrs. Irene motivated me to meet with a guidance counselor and strived to ensure school would be a safe, welcoming environment for me so I could escape the turmoil at home.

Overcoming my family's derailment would not have been possible without the other two members of my Golden Trio: Mackenzie and Emily. My best friends stayed by my side through thick and thin. They constantly reminded me to enjoy all the precious moments—ones overflowing with smiles, laughter, and happiness.

The Hartman family extended their support and gratitude beyond the roles of coach and teammate. They regularly checked on my family, brought meals to our house, and inspired me to apply the lessons and strength I acquired on the lacrosse field to my personal setbacks.

The Peyton family also deeply cared about us. Their love, care, and support make them one of the greatest families I have ever had the pleasure to know. I am grateful for the numerous times Mrs. Peyton and their youngest daughter picked me and Emma—the oldest daughter—up from lacrosse and dropped me off at home. The fifteen-minute drive from school to my house was often the best and most comforting moment of my day. The Peyton family reminded me of the importance of living my best life by enjoying the moments we have together.

Lastly, my aunt and my godparents showed me immeasurable grace. My aunt was always ready to help me and my family, no matter the time of day. She focused on making sure I was okay and received all the necessary care I needed, whether it was getting to lacrosse practice on time, attending a friend's birthday party, or eating a meal. My godparents invited me to escape the rolling hills of Pittsburgh for a week of rest, recharging, and fun that I almost passed up because I initially thought I did not deserve it. All three of them cared for me and loved me like a daughter.

Gratitude is one of the most powerful, uplifting, and healthy emotions. It allows you to acknowledge all the good we already have and will receive in our lives. Personally, throughout and beyond my dad's cancer diagnosis, I have felt incredibly grateful and unbelievably blessed. Gratitude has become one of my positive affirmations, allowing me to see the good things in this world and appreciate all the gifts and benefits I receive every moment.

CHAPTER 11

AUTHENTICITY

"If you can't see anything beautiful about yourself, get a better mirror, look a little closer, stare a little longer. Because there is something inside of you that made you keep trying despite everyone who told you to quit." [36]

—SHANE KOYCZAN

As the only woman on her company's supply chain management team, Katie has pushed the limits of what is possible while continually staying true to herself. On several occasions, she experienced harassment at work. She was a victim of frequent mansplaining—when a man talks to a woman in a manner that is considered patronizing—and the butt of jokes that the male employees shared among themselves. Although they eventually resolved the situation, she found working through this challenge to be exceedingly difficult. Katie's work environment made her feel worthless,

36 *TED*, "'To This Day' ... for the Bullied and Beautiful | Shane Koyczan," March 8, 2013, video, 12:03.

diminished her confidence, and revealed how her coworkers often willfully ignored her.

Additionally, Katie was the only woman to double major in marketing and supply chain management and co-lead the Supply Chain Management Club at her university. She was frequently told by her male classmates that supply chain was a "boys club" and no women were allowed. They told her she should stick to majoring in marketing.

Katie knew to not take those comments seriously, yet she could not help feeling discouraged that her own classmates did not believe she belonged or was capable of pursuing her career. Eventually, she approached one of her supply chain professors about the situation. The professor told Katie her fellow classmates' attitudes were not going to get them anywhere in life. After sharing with her professor the peer pressure and the struggles she had experienced, Katie suddenly realized she shouldn't quit her career passion.

"There is always something you can learn from every moment and opportunity, even if it goes completely south," Katie stated in a conversation with me. "At the end of the day, if you are true to yourself, you're going to have a positive outcome and it'll pay off in the long run, whether it's today or tomorrow."

The lesson Katie learned from the conversation with her supply chain professor about upholding her authenticity became applicable in traversing another challenge. In her four-year undergraduate career, Katie served in a variety of leadership roles on executive boards. The leadership in these organizations ranged from fantastic to toxic, where members blamed her for problems and piled tasks on her.

On these pernicious executive boards, she found some of the older students took advantage of her and ran the organization like a dictatorship. The leaders on these poorly run executive boards wanted Katie to follow their lead and conform to their specific style of leadership, attitudes, and beliefs. They wanted Katie to change herself and what she believed so she could fit in with the crowd.

Despite the setbacks and the constant peer pressure, Katie never gave up. She continually pushed for what she knew was right and stayed true to herself. She revealed to me one of her biggest takeaways from her collegiate years that has allowed her to become the best version of herself:

"Don't ever lose your voice, your authentic self, or your confidence. You have it, you are born with it, and it's what makes you, *you*!" Katie shared. "Don't let people take that away from you and don't think for one instant that it isn't important enough to matter in your life!"

What I admire about Katie's story is that her commitment to being authentic did not waver during challenges from her coursework, leadership roles, and profession. In fact, the challenges created stronger reinforcements within her to become the best version of herself and to persevere onward.

* * *

Authenticity is about answering the question, "Who am I?" It is defined as trusting who you are, being your unique self, and seeing your unlimited potential. It is about having full confidence in your capabilities, values, morals, and beliefs. Embodying authenticity is a process that requires deep introspection of your most sincere thoughts and feelings, acknowledging your development, and discovering what motivates you.

To embrace authenticity requires living the life you genuinely want to live rather than living the life others expect of you or think you are supposed to live. When looking inward and examining who we are, we tend to scrutinize ourselves, becoming our own harshest critic. We doubt our capabilities and accomplishments, constantly beating ourselves up and comparing ourselves to others. The American Psychological Association describes this common phenomenon of self-doubt and criticism as "imposter syndrome"—the psychological motive of severe inadequacy and self-doubt that leaves people fearing they are a fraud or a failure.[37]

Imposter syndrome is the opposite of being your authentic self. It makes us think we are worthless, gives us unrealistic expectations, and covers us in blemishes and wounds that make us lose our sense of purpose. On a few occasions, I, too have fallen into the trap of imposter syndrome. My dad has always wanted me to be my authentic self; however, upon promising my father I would continue to excel in school and lacrosse for him, the onset of fear burned within me. I feared

---

37 Lydia Craig, "Are You Suffering from Imposter Syndrome? Ways to Identify and Deal with Feelings of Self-Doubt in Grad School," *American Psychological Association*, September 2018.

I might not live up to his expectations or uphold his wishes. I downplayed my academic capabilities despite having an impressive track record.

Furthermore, my self-doubt started burying me alive because I strove for an unreachable, subjective goal of being perfect. Automatically assuming I was not good enough or didn't think it was possible to continue to excel in school despite my circumstances was nauseating. Yet, with my intentions set on seeing how my dad's cancer could positively transform our lives, I knew I could not let my love for learning falter.

School was a haven, a sanctuary, and a gift where I got to socialize with my friends and fill my mind with knowledge. It distracted me by giving me various assignments and introducing new subjects I immediately dived into. Learning gave me piece of mind, allowing me to be my authentic self and feel wholesome, content, and overjoyed. A passion for learning is not everyone's cup of tea, but it's what I value and makes me unique.

* * *

Shortly after my dad's diagnosis, I scheduled an appointment with the high school counseling center despite having no prior experience meeting with a counselor before. When I arrived at the threshold of the counseling office, I took in the new surroundings. The bright morning light broke through the cheap blinds. The walls were a soft baby blue, covered haphazardly with various photographs, awards, and inspirational quotes. Across from where I stood was a desk with stacks of papers and files. To the right was a table with snacks and candy next to two cushioned chairs. Only one of those chairs was vacant—my guidance counselor sat in the other.

"Hi, you must be Nicole. Have a seat." The tone of their voice was reassuring. They smiled as they readjusted their reading glasses.

I wasted no time walking over to the remaining, empty chair. I slung the strap of my tote over my seat and slid a few books under my chair. Then, I divulged the recent circumstances that had invaded my life. My counselor paused and digested what I shared. They thanked me for sharing this sensitive information with them and continued the conversation in a calming manner.

"It's challenging to comprehend such a reality when our community lives in a bubble. It seems that you and your family are about to embark on an extraordinary journey like no other, given the severity and rareness of your father's diagnosis."

I kept my head bowed, periodically closing my eyes to build up enough courage to withstand this dreaded yet imperative conversation. My counselor continued,

"You do know that is why we're here—the faculty. We have a duty to support our students, even beyond the classroom and the scope of the subjects we teach. All of this has you visibly upset and in a state of shock, I presume."

As my guidance counselor spoke, I fought to regain control over myself and reassure my nerves someone was merely scratching the surface of what consists in my day-to-day life.

"Before I continue, I would like to know what *you want.*"

I thought I wanted everything to go back to normal and that this never happened to my family. I thought I wanted to escape the suffering that was choking me. Part of me did, but there was also a fire burning inside of me that wanted something else . . .

I raised my head and without shedding a tear, I replied to my counselor with the utmost reassurance,

"I love school and learning. It is part of what makes me, me. I am willing to strive to achieve the education that I desire because I have immense plans and dreams in my future. I don't want anything to come between me and learning."

Pausing for a moment to regain more strength to release what was truly on my mind, I continued.

"I want my teachers to realize that despite my circumstances, I'm still willing to put forth the time and effort into the coursework. I'm the least likely student in this school to slack off or become lazy."

I had to take a few breaths and swallow my anxiety to finish concluding my thoughts. "School is probably the one thing that could make my father proud of me . . . to stay determined to beat this cancer . . . because I promised him."

I felt weightless for quite some time after verbalizing my thoughts. My counselor remained silent and still, gently nodding.

They finally spoke, "School is a remarkable, unappreciated gift as well as a good escape from the chaos at home. I have full faith that the rest of the faculty will accommodate you in any way possible."

I beamed with pride and hope, albeit a mere sliver. I walked out of the guidance counselor's office feeling like I was walking on a cloud—at least temporarily—as some of my burden lifted off my shoulders. I came to the realization that I needed to cut myself some slack, embrace my genuine imperfections, and strive to be the best version of *myself.*

Although apprehensive at first, I found conversing with my guidance counselor about my dad's cancer and my personal concerns to be remarkably reassuring. I was relieved to know the high school faculty would recognize and appreciate my determination to do well in school so I could continue to be authentically myself. After my appointment with the counselor, my teachers suggested practical and manageable solutions that allowed me to excel in school despite my family's derailment. Having a comforting place to talk about my intentions, situation, recurring thoughts, and feelings helped me make a comeback and released some of the burden I carried on my shoulders.

* * *

It was initially frustrating to overcome obstacles while dealing with being a young woman, garnering confidence, and maintaining my authentic identity. Yet in that moment, sitting in a private room away from the halls filled with peer pressure, bullying, and intimidation, I discovered I was still

Nicole—only stronger, wiser, and better. I knew who I was, what I loved, and what I dreamt of would not vanish out of my reach. I knew I could keep the promise I made to my dad about staying true to my authentic self and doing well in both school and lacrosse.

My authenticity proved to be exceptionally important in shaping me into the woman I'm proud to be today. Focusing on academics gave me a reason to celebrate small wins and accomplishments. Ultimately, doing well in school was something I was proud of and gave me something to look forward to each day during the years to come.

My high school experience gave me the aspiration to seek the world beyond the walls of a provincial life. It reminded me to seize every opportunity to learn something new about myself and the world, to discover what pulls at my heart strings, and follow what leads me toward my life's purpose. Ensuring my education would not falter because of uncontrollable circumstances allowed me to explore the greatest benefits of having an education: further discovering who I am and finding a professional passion.

I recognize and celebrate my self-worth, for my reflection reveals a beautiful, limitless, wonderful, smart, creative, strong, and capable young woman. I know all my extraordinary experiences made my life richer and what I attained during these circumstances—the positive and the traumatic—were the keys that unlocked my true identity and potential. My dad's battle with cancer refined my courage, patience, and passion to go the distance and make a difference.

For me, authenticity was not about finding myself; it was about growing to become a version of myself who was braver, more enlightened, and happier.

Being authentic is a freeing experience that allows me to emerge from hiding and enjoy life as the genuine Nicole. Working on myself from the inside out allows me to overcome insecurities and self-destructive behaviors that imposter syndrome loves so dearly.

Like being authentic, your story is unique and incomparable; you are the only one who can write it and the one who needs to hear it most.

You are the protagonist of your story and you experience all the plot twists. Authenticity instilled in me the confidence to tell my story and to uncover the values and lessons that would propel me through my life's setbacks. By staying true to who I am and believing in myself, I know there is not anything in life I cannot handle. By embracing authenticity, I can simultaneously be a badass and my unapologetic self.

CHAPTER 12

SELF-CARE

"Self-care is so important. When you take the time to replenish your spirit, it allows you to serve others from the overflow. You can't serve from an empty vessel." [38]

—ELEANOR BROWNN

Inconsistency was Colin's sense of normalcy. Growing up, Colin was affected by his father's behaviors related to bipolar—or manic—depression. In a matter of a few days, his father would go from being happy and healthy to ill and lacking interest in his life. Colin became extremely divided in his feelings toward his dad: he loved his father, but it was challenging to engage with him during his lowest lows. Becoming the "man of the house" for his mom and sister, Colin struggled to maintain a strong family dynamic while simultaneously dealing with his college coursework and adjusting to the working world.

38 "Most Popular Quotes by Eleanor Brownn," Eleanor Brownn, accessed August 26, 2020.

In the midst of transitional periods in his life, Colin wished he had a male role model to admire or ask for guidance. He deeply wanted a stronger father-son relationship; however, in his junior year of college, Colin came to embody the qualities of the role model he always wanted.

"I found that discovering things that boosted my overall self-care allowed me to persevere through my academics and extracurricular activities," Colin shared. "It definitely took time, patience, and energy to find the right balance and discover what was lifting me up toward progress or pulling me down toward a setback."

After many months of practicing self-care, prioritizing his physical health, and attending regular sessions with counseling professionals, Colin still felt burdened by all his stressors. Distress and pressure were leading Colin in a direction in life that he did not want. Through deep reflection and self-evaluation, Colin realized there are a multitude of ways to practice self-care and he could change what did not work. He decided assisting others who are enduring similar circumstances empowered him to properly cope with his persistent worries and his dad's mental illness.

"As a passion aside from my financial advisor position, I started volunteering at the Cornerstone of Hope, a center that helps young adults work through the grieving process after a loss and shows them how to cope with unfortunate setbacks," Colin explained. "I serve on the board of directors and oversee the various committees so I can help spark greater awareness and gain support for our efforts and programming."

Volunteering at Cornerstone of Hope reinforced the idea that to help others cope through their losses and stressors, Colin had to prioritize taking care of himself first. Since starting at Cornerstone of Hope, Colin has become happier, more stable, and better able to support both himself and his family. By continually reinforcing self-care practices, Colin has become a role model for others who wish to let go of what is holding them back from living.

"I've found enjoyment helping other people cope with uncertainty and discover a more meaningful life that awaits them," said Colin. "Finding ways to uphold and prioritize our self-care makes getting through the everyday frustrations and worries we face easier to overcome."

* * *

Colin's story demonstrates how actively engaging in activities that promote your mental, emotional, and physical health is crucial and how prioritizing self-care means putting your well-being first every day—not just when you're feeling under the weather. Self-care is an affirmative, ceaseless experience of health, happiness, and prosperity of which you are in control, allowing you to feel and be well.

Self-care is a subjective concept and there is no single definition for this term, but most agree it includes the presence of positivity, the absence of negative emotions, satisfaction with life, fulfillment, and effective functioning. According to *Harvard Business Review,* although there are infinite opportunities for personal growth, self-care, and stress relief, what makes practicing self-care challenging for some people is it requires us to take a genuine break from goal-oriented and metric-driven thinking.[39]

There is no one-size-fits-all approach to maintaining and demonstrating an affirmative relationship with oneself because self-care means different things to different people. Some people see that taking a nap periodically and sticking to a nutritious diet may work for them. Others may benefit best from applying a face mask or devoting a day to step away from all screens and technology.

> Regardless of what healthy practices you prefer, self-care shouldn't be considered a selfish act; it's about knowing what we truly need to properly take care of ourselves and live a more balanced life.

I have always been physically healthy but prevailing through my dad's battle with cancer showed me there was more to my health and longevity than just my body. After the diagnosis, my mental and emotional health suffered as I struggled to find mechanisms to effectively manage the overwhelming stress of my dad's illness. On a few occasions, I broke into tears unexpectedly from feeling overwhelmed. The stress and negativity attempted to break down my mind and body like a wrecking ball.

---

39 Charlotte Lieberman, "How Self-Care Becomes So Much Work," *Harvard Business Review*, August 10, 2018.

I had a few of my close friends tell me "Nicole, you deserve to take a step back away from your stressors."

After accidentally snapping at my brother for hounding me about all the details from our dad's surgery, he replied gingerly, "You shouldn't be carrying this heavy burden by yourself . . . you need to rest up and take time for you, sis."

Every time I stormed up to my room in frustration when I felt incapable of helping my dad, I would often ask myself:

"How can I make time to enjoy the little things in life and the remaining threads of my youth? How can I devote time for me in the midst of all this?"

How I prioritized and took care of myself translated into how I cared for my family. If I didn't take care of myself, I might have become irritable while helping my dad, not been able to support him if he was in pain, and lack the strength to overcome the challenges to discover all the good ahead. Unfortunate circumstances can produce recurring feelings of grief, negativity, and suffering while also sparking triggers that forcibly steer us downhill. We can control these dampening setbacks and find ways to boost our wellness, move forward beyond the current moment, and be better equipped for the next challenge.

To take better care of my overall health, I became actively engaged in self-care activities. Self-care allowed me to recharge so I could establish a stronger, healthier relationship with myself. Additionally, it gave me free range to push the boundaries of creativity, increase my confidence, and improve my self-esteem.

Self-care reminds me to do things that make me feel more like myself and encourages me to explore new things.

Balancing stress and satisfaction are life's biggest roller coaster rides. Self-care is a personal growth journey and improvement that happens over time. Throughout my family's life-altering hurdle and my wellness journey, I have found many of my daily, routine, self-care activities became effective coping mechanisms to help me survive life's unpredictable storms. My self-care techniques have evolved over time as I discovered more along my life's journey; however, there are three noteworthy self-care practices I capitalize upon so I can further enjoy my life and feel more like me. They allowed me to work on myself for me.

* * *

My first method of self-care is writing and journaling, which allows me to digest and process every detail, thought, feeling, behavior, and moment I experience. These details and thoughts fill the blank pages of my journals and tell my story. I also used my journals for things such as learning, drawing, brainstorming ideas, and remembering positive affirmations. I have always loved to write, but during my dad's diagnosis I learned how writing can serve as a self-reflection technique. Transferring my worries out of my mind and onto paper allowed me to acknowledge my thoughts and emotions. I felt lighter, happier, and at ease.

My writing also transcended above journals and stationery. Ever since I was seven years old, my grandmother and I have been pen pals. To this day, we write each other handwritten, cursive letters every week. Integrating journaling and letter writing into my daily routine was a seamless way to capture and reflect on the precious details of my life's moments.

When we write about our stressors, we transform our mindset and gain new insights, reveal our humanity to others, and communicate authentically. Writing a children's book version of my dad's battle with cancer for a school project was perhaps one of the hardest and most rewarding projects I have ever completed. Recalling all those heartbreaking moments was not easy to swallow yet writing about my family's situation healed me. Every word I wrote and every detail I shared released the many months of pressure and anxiety I longed to release. Putting all those moments together into my book made me appreciate just how far my family had come. Writing our story showed me that it was not a tragedy—it was a rebirth!

* * *

The second of my self-care methods is reading. Books enrich my mind and grant me temporary escape from reality; they allow me to wander into wonder, observe the surrounding world, invoke my inner child, and dream about adventures into marvelous worlds beyond our universe. I resonate with numerous characters as they embark on extraordinary adventures through Middle Earth or into a wardrobe and accrue meaningful life lessons. Personally, I find after reading a chapter, listening to the original score of the film adaptation of a book, or pretending to relive a scene in my mind that the lessons my beloved characters acquire are applicable to overcoming my life's setbacks, too.

I have and will always be an avid fan of the *Harry Potter* series. The seven books shined the brightest light for me during the dark times of my life, including during my dad's severe diagnosis. Harry himself taught me to never give up as he endured battles throughout the series and persevered through all of them. He showed me I can push through even the hardest of times, bounce back, and succeed. Hermione Granger became a role model of mine, proving a woman is worthy and beyond capable of being educated, becoming a warrior, and facing her fears.

Harry Potter reminded me that sometimes the only way is the hardest way, but it's during these times that we find out who we really are and what we're capable of. The life lessons books have taught me have instilled within me the determination to see where my life's adventure will take me and to seek what is out there waiting for me.

* * *

Finally, running became a way to momentarily escape my circumstances, release negativity, and battle alongside my dad to beat the cancer. I needed to run fast for an extended duration of time when playing my midfielder position in sports such as soccer, lacrosse, and field hockey. Running was in the family; Corey and my dad both ran cross country and track and field in high school and ran in half marathons as adults. For as long as I can remember, my dad would wake up early every morning and run five miles through our neighborhood. Unfortunately, after his surgery, he was not able to run for several months. Seeing how much my dad missed running and wished to regain his strength, I made it my mission to run each day for him.

Running in suburban Pittsburgh is no easy feat. The rolling hills, massive bridges, unpaved bendy roads, and sharp turns I covered accurately depicted and symbolized the ups and downs of hurdling life's mountainous obstacles; each hill I climbed, meadow I explored, or bridge I crossed represented a setback I overcame. While I ran, the crisp morning air would rid my mind of recurring negative thoughts. The habit of running every day was a freeing experience; each step and each breath propelled me forward as I surpassed my opponent: my dad's cancer. After all that time spent running in his place, it was rewarding to see my dad run again, and even better to run alongside him.

On the path of continuous healing, I take the self-care strategies I found beneficial and used them to propel myself onward. I have learned to place self-care on the top of my to-do list every day. Self-care is an investment you make in yourself. It requires small, incremental changes that allows your light to shine brightly. From self-care, I have learned coping mechanisms improve my overall well-being and found the confidence to face the stress head-on. Consistently practicing self-care has set me on a path to be the happiest and healthiest version of myself. It is a unique journey that allows me to actively live the life I want to live while simultaneously respecting, loving, and valuing myself.

PART III

CONTINUOUS GROWTH AND THE LIVING PROOF

CHAPTER 13

JUST KEEP GROWING, GROWING, GROWING

The personal stories in this book that captured moments of sacrifice, stress, and difficulty have evolved into self-discoveries, happiness, creativity, and intrinsic capabilities. Within their lives thus far, each person I interviewed created their own path and consciously chose to fully embody the building blocks needed to overcome their setbacks and unveil their true potential. These building blocks became the stepping stones they pushed off from to close the gap between their circumstances and their beyond.

These building blocks (gaining perspective, vulnerability and transparency, resiliency, compassion, adaptability, gratitude, authenticity, and self-care) have not only become necessities, but also game-changing capabilities for those overcoming life obstacles to make greater comebacks. You can simultaneously leverage these intertwined concepts, although you may use some of the building blocks more often than others at different points in time. These building blocks are always with us, surrounding us throughout life's moments. They strengthen our inner abilities to hurdle over our setbacks, recover from our discomfort, and recognize that our challenges are teachable moments that allow us to go beyond and prevail in future circumstances.

Vulnerability and transparency granted Nick the courage to openly share his thoughts and feelings with his family, doctors, and friends during his recovery from the removal of his brain tumor. Becoming adaptable may have been a requirement for Marissa growing up in a military family, but it gave her the patience to go with the flow and discover bigger, better opportunities waiting for her. Christian unearthed countless ways that his extremely rare cancer turned into a wake-up call that encouraged him to live a grateful, meaningful life while walking closer to God.

These building blocks are lessons we learn by overcoming obstacles, and we can apply them later in life when facing challenges. We all have the potential to embrace them and capitalize on them. Utilizing the building blocks as new challenges arise will optimize your life and open the doors to new opportunities. The result of learning and implementing the building blocks throughout the ups and downs of life is continuous growth.

For me, continuous growth emphasizes that life is about the *quality of our journey*, not the destination. Our journeys are ever-lengthening, ever-ascending, and ever-improving paths; they take you on spectacular adventures to find your inner potential, identify your interests and values, set your intentions, and strive toward achieving long-term goals and dreams. Your growth and recovery cannot be done in random spurts of energy or all at once, but through long-term, gradual progression.

Embarking on your continuous growth journey requires you to trust where you are; the challenges you are facing right now are preparing you for what is to come. Obstacles will attempt to disrupt your dreams and knock you down, but you will find a way to overcome and rise above them using the building blocks.

We can get right back up again, face our setbacks, and go beyond them.

We have been given many chances to learn from our circumstances and to grow through what we have gone through.

* * *

To further illustrate the idea of continuous growth toward one's beyond by embodying the building blocks, I will tell Sarah's story.

Freshman year of college, Sarah became inseparable from her randomly assigned roommate, Emily. They did everything together; no matter where one went, the other was not too far behind. Their friendship flourished and they lived together for two and a half years. However, in one moment, everything changed.

According to witnesses, medical professionals, and family, on October 11, 2015, Sarah drove down a highway with

Emily in the passenger seat. Another car hit them from behind, causing their car to spin out of control and hit a median.

Emily died on the scene.

Sarah was life-flighted to a local hospital in critical condition. At the hospital, the nurses asked Sarah if she knew where she was or how she got here. Groggy and in pain, Sarah did not know what had happened—she did not remember anything. She had no idea she was driving a car let alone that Emily had been with her and did not survive. When the nurses and her family shared the unfortunate news, Sarah broke down. All the information hit her all at once and she struggled to digest it all, all Sarah could think about was that her college roommate and best friend was lost, gone in a flash.

"The hardest part about losing Emily was that I wanted to talk to her," Sarah shared. "We talked about everything and anything together. Realizing that she wasn't here anymore when I needed her most was heartbreaking."

Upon being released from the hospital, Sarah's small university was more than accommodating and allowed her to finish the semester from home without having to medically withdraw or postpone her graduation. Despite her absence from campus, news of the accident spread like wildfire. Suddenly, Sarah became known as "the girl who was in a car accident." Being constantly associated with the traumatic event made it even harder for Sarah to move forward. During her recovery and initial grieving stage, Sarah reflected on how she was determined to not let this situation define her and figure out what she should do next.

"I knew that if Emily were here, she would be so upset to find out that I was moping around all the time. She would want me to get out of bed every morning and find a way to be happy again," Sarah stated.

Sarah is still close with Emily's family. They continually keep in touch and support each other. One day Emily's dad told Sarah, "You are here for some reason, Sarah . . . go discover what awaits you," which proved to be a transformative moment for Sarah.

Rather than letting the terrible event consume her, Sarah made the conscious decision to make the best of that situation and allow it to shape her life's journey. The accident was a learning experience to discover more about herself, where her strengths lie, and what she truly wants in life.

"I learned a lot of hard lessons: acceptance, being self-sufficient, and resilience. Just because things did not go your way doesn't mean you have any right to give up," Sarah admitted. "I learned how to accept things the way they are now rather than the way they have been. Yeah, it sucks, but I knew that I was going to get through it and be okay. I figured out how to get through these challenging moments."

Putting one foot in front of the other with renewed energy and stronger than ever before, Sarah decided to step out of her comfort zone to grow beyond that terrible moment. The semester after the crash, Sarah joined a sorority and not only met amazing people but also became immersed in a community she never knew she needed. Her new sisters respected her and the way she carried herself and saw how good, strong, and brave Sarah was.

"I got over that hump that was probably my lowest of lows. I acquired this new perspective of understanding how to be okay when things are not okay and grow from that experience. I figured out what I want and know I can achieve it. I can do anything that I set my heart and mind to!" Sarah exclaimed.

Through this unfortunate setback, Sarah learned that every one of us will go through something in our lives that will put us to the test and throw us a curveball that we never anticipated. Sarah's story shows that how we handle the situation, learn from it, and move beyond it will positively impact our journey.

* * *

Although Sarah didn't have a typical college experience and had to grow up extraordinarily fast, she found a way to make the most of every day, be happy in the moment, enjoy new relationships, and grow throughout and beyond the tragic moment. Having a powerful goal such as continuous growth to pursue during challenging times and throughout our lives will transform your life story into a masterpiece. Making the commitment to strive toward continuous growth regardless of what life brings your way sets you on your unique path of purposeful fulfillment. Over time, you will be able to live your life to the fullest and become your own living proof that we can thrive beyond life's moments.

I am convinced temporary, stressful setbacks with seemingly no end in sight opened my eyes to see the real me, what my capabilities are, and what's in store for me in the years to come. Through my dad's battle with cancer, I acquired my confidence, instilled determination, and materialized the eight comprehensive building blocks. Initially, I didn't think I had the courage to share the children's book I wrote about my dad with him, the perseverance to lead the comeback during my lacrosse game, the determination to fight cancer alongside my dad, or the patience to wait over twelve hours in the hospital wondering if I would see my dad again. Nevertheless, I managed to continually put the building block concepts in motion, leading me on the charge to prevail during my dad's cancer derailment and throughout my life to this day.

Although my dad finished his radiation treatments and started to run again, he had more appointments, examinations, and minor treatments throughout the rest of my high school years, which brewed stress and discomfort. He still deals with the ramifications of losing his sense of smell, not being able to generate an adequate amount of saliva and having extreme sensitivities with his nose. Yet, by instilling the building blocks during the initial year of my dad's diagnosis, they have now become second nature to me, making the lingering aftermath of my dad's surgery manageable to work through. They became applicable in situations beyond my family's encounter with cancer: in the classroom, on the varsity field, during a run, and in the blank pages of a journal.

The eight building blocks and the continuous growth mindset provide a framework for how to live a purposeful live and strive toward your true potential. Your transformation of growing through and beyond your life obstacles puts you on the path to fully engage with and immerse yourself in the purpose you are meant to live out. We all have a purpose—the deep reason for our existence—that is greater than ourselves. Your purpose exists in the beyond; it shifts and evolves throughout your life and your own experiences while giving our life meaning and fulfillment. To go beyond and live out your purpose, you have to overcome your setbacks, constantly grow, and learn from your triumphs and mistakes.

Our purpose in life does not have to always be this grand mission or require an out-of-this-world discovery. Our purpose can be related to a profession, vocation, charitable cause, or simply a way of living day-by-day.

Continuous growth also attracts a multitude of opportunities for you. Each opportunity you seize is one step closer to unveiling your authentic potential. It does not happen all at once; the small intentions you make each day to be a better version of yourself will get you one step closer to your greater purpose in life.

* * *

As I reflect on my life and examine the lives of those who have inspired me, I have realized our challenges deserve some more credit. Overcoming obstacles did not slow down my progress or my life—it *enhanced* my experiences and future opportunities. Handling my family's cancer derailment and other challenges helped me identify what I wanted to do, where I wanted to be, and what I found to be important to me.

My challenges have rekindled and sparked new relationships, strengthened my Catholic faith, identified my values and interests, revealed my passions, and guided me to pursuing a career in Human Resources.

Throughout the implementation of the building blocks and continuous growth, overcoming obstacles can not only transform our personal lives as we aim toward going beyond—they can light the path toward discovering our passions, purpose, and professions.

Working through her panic attacks and mental health battles, Angela received a purposeful call to action: to serve her community and campus through the roles of a Peer Health Advocate and an EMT with the hopes of becoming either a surgical oncologist or a physician's assistant. Colin became a role model for other young adults dealing with grief and loss at the Cornerstone of Hope after not having a true father-son relationship and carrying his family's burden for over twenty years. Being authentic rather than succumbing to peer pressure gave Katie all the strength she needed to pursue her ambitions in supply chain management and break down professional barriers.

Angela, Colin, Katie, and countless others who have overcome a variety of life obstacles found a way to shine the light amid their challenges to reveal wonderful opportunities both personally and professionally.

I bet now you can comprehend why other inspiring individuals and I have viewed their distressing setbacks as wonderful gifts to be thankful for.

How we choose to perceive, prevail through, and grow from our stressful circumstances can directly impact our happiness, relationships, careers, and purpose.

During my life, I have been fortunate to have met incredible people who have instilled the building block concepts and who have continually grown during and beyond their circumstances. Everyone highlighted in the pages of these chapters is truly inspiring, but I still have three stories that have yet to be told. These last stories are about role models who explicitly illustrate why continuous growth is the key to overcoming obstacles and discovering your purpose. Along with these stories, I will share how the building blocks and continuous growth mindset were essential throughout my collegiate experiences and in my profession.

Although we are approaching the final chapters of this book, the journey has just commenced. Keep striving to rise high above your setbacks and never look back. You have new mountains to climb in front of you and huge ambitions to achieve. No matter what you are currently going through, always know there is so much to look forward to. There is a beyond, and you are on your way to getting there.

CHAPTER 14

THREE TRANSFORMATIONAL TESTIMONIES

I have been graciously blessed with some incredible people in my life who continually amaze me. Like me, several of these people have positively viewed their uncertain derailments and, in turn, unlocked their beyond.

I have witnessed their transformations firsthand. I have documented their stories to inspire you.

KELSEY: FROM ASPIRING DOCTOR TO MAGNIFICENT DREAMER

Kelsey felt like she had been stumbling blindly through her academic life, passions, hobbies, and social situations for the past twenty-four years, just trying to figure out her life.

People always told her she was "gifted," which had both perks and downfalls. Kelsey hardly ever studied, but still managed earn top honors. Her intelligence made her a target of bullying, which negatively impacted her mental health and caused her to experience social isolation. Rather than spending time with kids her own age, Kelsey devoted her downtime to creative interests and passions like dance, nature, learning, and the magic of Disney.

Kelsey grew up in a culturally sheltered household in a rural community with a long family lineage of healthcare professionals, and her parents pressured their children to carry out this family legacy. During her freshman year of high school, Kelsey committed herself to being a doctor—specifically, an oncologist because of her fascination with biology, natural sciences, and cancer.

Kelsey's journey to become a doctor began at a private university where she majored in Biology and minored in Population and Public Health. During her junior year of college, Kelsey realized she was developing some serious mental health issues—possibly either generalized or social anxiety due to not socializing enough as a child. Her realization came after experiencing symptoms of anxiety that she had never felt before during her first two and a half years in college.

"I was more anxious than ever before; I was gasping for air in my organic chemistry classes, crying over biochemistry notes, and hyperventilating at the thought of physics class," Kelsey explained. "Yet, I loved learning about global health systems, etiology, and everything related to nature with a driving passion."

Halfway through her junior year, Kelsey started going to the counseling center for assistance with stress management, then started therapy for general anxiety during her senior year. Every single counseling or therapy session Kelsey attended not only gave her the tools she needed to prioritize self-care and keep her brain healthy and on track, but also provided her with the confidence and ability to speak up for herself regarding her personal happiness and future.

* * *

By the spring of 2018, Kelsey managed to push through the hardships she experienced during her courses to graduate with honors. She had given up on medical school after having an anxiety attack in front of her parents while discussing her future over her summer before her senior year. Kelsey's next plan was to become a physical therapist; however, she still was not sure about what she really wanted to do in her future. Through deep reflection, Kelsey became transparent and vulnerable with herself, realizing the two things she genuinely wanted in her career: to enjoy work and to help others.

"As much as I am grateful for having a strong sense of intelligence, I didn't love my status of being 'gifted' enough to sacrifice my own happiness," shared Kelsey. "I wanted to find a job that allowed me to use my intelligence *and* my creativity while allowing myself to find joy in my job."

In November 2018, the Disney College Program accepted Kelsey as an Attractions Cast Member for the Spring 2019 cohort. Shortly after starting at Disney, Kelsey discovered while working at Expedition Everest and Kali River Rapids how animal sciences, environmental studies, and conservation education are used in several attractions at Disney. Suddenly, during her internship, Kelsey realized she could blend her two biggest passions seamlessly: Disney and biology.

"I came to Disney World not really knowing what it would have in store for me and thought I would go with the flow and see where the opportunity would take me. This internship helped me overcome the hardships I experienced in my past," Kelsey explained. "I learned much more during the one year that I worked for the Walt Disney Company than I could have ever imagined. Not only are there tremendous opportunities to grow and advance here, but Disney also places more emphasis on treating others with compassion and listening to their stories rather than someone's intelligence."

Recently, Kelsey accepted a position to stay at the Walt Disney Company as a part-time Attractions Cast Member with a goal of working up to a higher position within either the Conservation Education, Animal Sciences, or Environmental teams.

Kelsey's journey has led her to understand that she does not have to have her whole life figured out by a certain age. By staying resilient and committed to working through her mental health issues and past hardships, Kelsey propelled herself forward to grow and discover the bright future ahead of her. Kelsey's transformative story provides context for how our own setbacks can raise the stage curtains to reveal our true calling and provide a path toward endless happiness.

"I am working on the things that bring me the highest levels of fulfillment," Kelsey declared. "I might never cure cancer as I

had once hoped, and that's okay. I can still make a difference and live a purposeful life—if it is only by making myself happy by doing what I want to do for a living, then so be it. At least I know that I am finally living my dream. Go out and do what makes you happy."

KLAIRE: FINDING INFINITE REASONS TO STAY AND ENJOY LIFE'S MOMENTS

Growing up, Klaire's life revolved around spending time with her mom's side of the family. She has four aunts, her grandma, Nana, and more than twenty cousins. Nana was a prevalent role-model for Klaire and the core of her mom's family. When Klaire was in eighth grade, Nana ended up in the hospital. While her mom and sister attended a meeting with one of Nana's primary doctors, Klaire found herself alone in Nana's hospital room, keeping her company while she was asleep.

In the stillness of the stuffy hospital room, Nana abruptly awoke, startling Klaire. She said, "I just wish my daughters would get along."

After saying those words, Nana immediately fell asleep as if nothing had happened.

Those were Nana's last words. On January 8, 2010, she passed away.

Within a few moments of her passing, World War III commenced right there in the hospital wing, with Klaire's mom and her four aunts fighting. Their loud voices reverberated throughout the building.

"I was in total shock," Klaire admitted. "I spent 90 percent of my life looking up to these women and then suddenly seeing their true colors, behaving this way in public, and listening to their arguments was exceedingly difficult."

Jealousy and anger brewed among the five sisters as they struggled to grieve in healthy ways, fought over the decisions made within the will, and blamed each other for taking things of significant value from their childhood home like their father's Vietnam War medals.

As Klaire listened to these arguments, she replayed Nana's last words in her mind. She realized she had to be the one to repair the shattered pieces of her family, thinking Nana might have said those last words to her specifically for a reason. Klaire took on a solo mission: bringing her family back together.

* * *

As soon as Klaire started Catholic high school, her mom and aunts sold Nana's house, stopped fighting, and ceased all communication, gatherings, and affection. After continuously making conscious intentions, prayers, and efforts that failed to deliver positive results, Klaire felt like she was out of options and saw no way to achieve her mission of bringing the family back together.

Carrying this burden inflicted so much pain and suffering on Klaire that she planned to take her own life. As she made her way down to the basement to do so, a godly moment intercepted her plan.

"I felt God's presence in that room, telling me that I am worth it and to keep moving forward in life to find all the people, moments, and experiences waiting for me," Klaire shared.

Abandoning the plan to take her own life, Klaire immediately retreated to her room and solemnly promised herself she would not speak or think about this derailing moment again.

Grateful for this revelation, Klaire decided she needed to embrace a refreshing new outlook on life to improve her overall mental well-being. After graduating from high school, she found a new place to call home at her university. Klaire quickly discovered college was a prime opportunity to forget her past hardships, leverage her capabilities, and take risks. Klaire's new adventure included getting involved with Campus Ministry and Fraternity & Sorority Life, as well as finding people she could call her best friends and family.

One night, Klaire spent time chatting with one of her best friends in her sorority, Tara. For some reason, their topic of discussion was the Lifetime movie called *Cyberbully.* In one of the movie scenes, the main character attempts to take her own life by overdosing on pills after being a target of online bullying.

As the conversation turned to this specific moment in the movie, Tara openly stated, "I couldn't imagine ever taking my precious life away."

Hearing those words caused Klaire's heart to skip a beat. She had been determined to never tell anyone about her suicide attempt, yet Klaire was not only hiding this secret from her friends and family; she was hiding it from herself. Hiding her past contemplation of suicide made Klaire feel like an impostor with bottled up thoughts and feelings. In this unexpected, meaningful moment, Klaire found a silver lining and finally allowed herself to be vulnerable about her past to fully enjoy her life.

With a burst of courage, she admitted to Tara she had previously tried to commit suicide. Telling Tara what had happened in high school made Klaire realize she had not been vulnerable or authentic with herself. After telling Tara her secret, Klaire could heal from what she had been hiding and grow beyond her past setback so she could enjoy her collegiate experience.

"I spent too long hiding behind closed doors and now I have been presented with this opportunity to set my heart free of this burden I have carried on my shoulders for many years," Klaire explained.

* * *

By being honest about her past with her best friend and herself, Klaire began to recover from her mental health issues, gradually moved beyond those past moments and became fully immersed herself into all the wonderful opportunities her university had in store for her. Besides discovering strong friendships, the collegiate organizations Klaire was passionate about positively impacted her mental health and personal development, allowed her to find her authentic self, and to feel accepted. After four years at her university—the first place where she rebuilt herself and pieced together her past—Klaire found her true calling.

"Pursuing higher education as my profession comes from a place of wanting everyone during their prime years of their lives to feel like they matter and have a purpose," Klaire explained. "I want to give my students the opportunity to piece together their life stories to discover their true selves and capabilities."

Klaire's story illustrates how even in the darkest of times, light, joy, and optimism will always prevail; her light shined so brilliantly that she found a new home, became vulnerable about her past and rediscovered her authentic self. Klaire's perseverance showed her she had a future, a purpose, and opportunities to flourish and allowed her to move forward while positively serving herself and others.

"I stayed for reasons that I didn't know then but know now.
I stayed to tell one person after another my story.
I stayed to see my future and discover my purpose.
I stayed for my family and for the friends that I haven't met yet.
I stayed to teach myself how to be stronger, day-by-day.
I stayed for opportunities that I would have otherwise missed.
I stayed to prove that life is worth it; you are worth it: every person, every failure, every success, every road trip, every cup of coffee, every friendship, every storm and every paradise."

JASON: DISCOVERING HIS "WHY" TO GO THE DISTANCE THROUGHOUT LIFE'S JOURNEY

"It's a tough world out there and you need to do your very best in school."

Jason heard this in seventh grade during the Great Recession of 2008, which left his dad, mom, and mom's boyfriend jobless. In the midst of this economic turmoil, Jason embodied an underdog mentality and became driven by the belief that being 100 percent wasn't good enough. This outlook triggered the onset of his anxiety, depression, and medical complications.

In eighth grade, Jason dedicated all his effort and time into training to become the best football player, pushing himself to get into the best shape of his life. The beginning of Jason's journey as a high school football player took an unexpected turn when he dislocated his right shoulder during the season's first official practice.

Jason felt defeated by his injury, which required surgery. It seemed like all his hard work had been flushed away. After navigating his family's situation during the recession in his early adolescence, Jason felt like he always needed to be the best in all his activities. He thought he had to work harder, push beyond his limits, and achieve quantitative results at lightning speed.

Jason displayed this need to achieve by continuing to play football after recovering from his surgery.

During his senior year of high school, Jason was one of the football team captains. Before the start of the fourth game of the season, he gave the pre-game speech. He told his team, "Play every snap like it's your last game."

Little did he know, it would be his last game.

In the third quarter, Jason dislocated his right shoulder again. An ambulance came, and EMTs carried him off the field on a stretcher. He had to wear a sling for six weeks, underwent another surgery over the holidays, and completed six consecutive months of physical therapy right up to his high school graduation. Despite his last season of football ending suddenly, Jason expressed sincere gratitude that he could play four games during his senior year.

"The goal I had was to not let this injury destroy me like it did during my freshman year of high school," Jason shared with me. "I personally believe I achieved that."

* * *

As Jason embarked on the next phase of his journey—college—with his results-driven frame of mind, he seamlessly transferred his energy from football to extracurricular activities and academics. Upon stepping foot on campus, Jason tied his shoelaces even tighter and hit the ground running in a hyper-competitive environment. He immediately got involved at his university, serving as a cohort leader in his Business Honors Program, working in the Human Resources Department, engaging in multiple student leadership positions, and cofounding a student organization geared toward giving back to Veterans.

During his sophomore year of college, Jason endured a major concussion that blurred his vision and resulted in several weeks of social isolation. After a long recovery, he intently focused on getting a stellar internship and building his brand on LinkedIn. He landed an internship in Pittsburgh in the summer of 2018. However, after spending three months actively engaged in fantastic learning experiences, Jason still was not satisfied.

"Even after interning as a sophomore, I still wasn't happy or content. I felt that I needed to make more sacrifices to obtain what I wanted rather than what I needed," Jason admitted. "I wanted to leave a legacy behind . . . to put my university on the map and be the absolute best. I put an extraordinary amount of pressure on myself because I didn't want to be unemployed after college after seeing how hard it was on my family to land opportunities after the Great Recession."

Upon returning to his university for the fall semester, Jason's junior year of college became a broken record; he dealt with more head-related trauma and developed PTSD that carried into the summer of 2019.

"I felt like I was stuck in a hole that was getting deeper and deeper. I felt like I couldn't dig myself out of this relentless cycle," Jason shared with me. "Even though on paper I looked 'successful,' I was physically and emotionally exhausted. I wasn't fulfilled in my life."

Enduring the burdensome strain on his body and mind for far too long, Jason decided to attend some regular counseling sessions that summer.

One conversation in particular changed Jason's life. His counselor started out this specific session with an excellent analogy.

"Jason, do you know the average career of a running back in the NFL?"

"Sure! The top running backs play for seven to ten years if they can stay healthy," Jason stated.

"Okay . . . that's for the 'elite' running backs. What about the *average* running backs?"

"Probably two to three years due to the wear and tear on their body from the game of football," Jason replied.

"Why do you think that is?" asked Jason's counselor.

"Because they constantly give 110 percent by always sprinting away from vicious contact," replied Jason without question.

"Precisely! Now let's shift our focus to a marathon runner," the counselor advised. "How long do you think a person would be able to run marathons?

Silence filled the stuffy office that sweltering summer day. Jason was stumped with no definite answer or estimated guess to provide to his counselor. After some time, the counselor finally completed his sports analogy.

"Twenty to thirty years. That's the longevity of a marathon runner."

This amazing discovery sparked a pivotal realization for Jason that strengthened his ability to adapt to his current circumstances. It didn't matter whether he was playing football, studying for an exam, or collaborating on a project; he was severely depleting his mental, emotional and physical well-being, all because of impostor syndrome and his greatest fear that he would never be good enough.

"Through my counseling sessions and the discovery of sprinter mode versus marathon mode, I gained this new perspective on life, realizing that the pace at which I was living my life was causing me to self-destruct," Jason stated. "I was too competitive, didn't celebrate my 'wins,' and doubted my self-worth constantly. I never took the time to slow down and prioritize my self-care. Originally, I didn't emphasize self-care at all because it wasn't 'results driven' or quantitative in my eyes; it took me reaching my breaking point to understand how important it truly is."

With the coaching from his therapy sessions and the unyielding intentions he instilled, Jason's dynamic transformation bloomed that summer and throughout his senior year. While striving to be more vulnerable, resilient, and *his* best rather than *the* best, Jason has given back to other students through career counseling, enabling him to continually pay forward the lessons that inspire him and others to thrive during challenges.

After graduation, Jason joined an ambitious leadership cohort in the city of Pittsburgh and continues to pursue his passions in human resources. He has learned to never question his self-worth or capabilities to go beyond life's many setbacks.

After personally witnessing firsthand how Jason has transcended his setbacks, his story speaks volumes about how we are often the ones who get in our own way when prevailing our life circumstances and finding our "why." His contagious positivity and optimistic mindset glows brighter than the night skyline of the Steel City. The lessons Jason has learned through counseling created stronghold bridges to cross any obstacles, empowering Jason to reach his future aspirations and pursue his ever-evolving life journey.

"The adversity I experienced exposed my inner vulnerability; I was trying to be the *best instead of* my *best. By hyper-focusing solely on results, I was on the brink of self-destruction. Accepting my vulnerabilities and being comfortable sharing my story with others led me toward my personal and professional fulfillment."*

I am more than inspired by Kelsey, Klaire, and Jason. I feel transformed, empowered, and blown away by their capabilities to transcend their circumstances, own their stories, embody the building blocks, and harness the beauty of continuously growing in the face of adversity. Recognizing that light always prevails during our setbacks propelled all three of them forward to pursue their passions and true calling. They are living proof that we all have the ability to thrive throughout and beyond our circumstances, our challenges being the very thing that sparks our transformation to infinitely grow beyond life's moments.

It's because of the three of them and the rest of the interviewee heroes in my book that I finally decided to share my story within these very chapters.

CHAPTER 15

REWRITING OUR PROFESSIONAL NARRATIVES

The transformative narratives of Kelsey, Klaire, Jason, and the others shared within the pages of this book are validations that our life's setbacks, derailments, and stressors are often the best teachers. When working through challenges, the building blocks instill invaluable lessons within us about thriving in adversity, discovering what we are truly capable of, and finding what awaits us beyond these uncertain moments.

Each and every one of us has the ability to transform our obstacles into great life lessons, putting us in a state of constant learning and development.

We are not meant to infinitely endure pain, be stuck in the past, or be consumed by uncertainty and self-doubt. We have been *designed* to move through and surmount the challenges that cross our life's paths.

The lessons and capabilities we learn while overcoming our distressing experiences propel us to infinitely grow through and beyond these moments to discover the next chapters in our lives. Yet, we should not overlook recognizing that the eight building block concepts and the continuous growth mindset have significant, positive, and lasting relevance in our professions. This realization can empower us to aim for a fulfilling career and lead us toward pursuing our passions and finding our true potential.

I personally believe the building blocks and continuous growth philosophy can help us resolve professional challenges. Additionally, I theorize they can inspire employees and champion leaders and managers to capitalize upon their own experiences or challenges. Ultimately, they will allow companies to strategically strive for hiring and retaining purpose-driven employees, drive business and social impact, and cultivate a healthy, accepting, trusting, and transparent culture. I have conceptualized these well-informed theories, ideas, and recommendations thus far through my comprehensive coursework at John Carroll University, my professional experiences in Human Resources, and my observations over the years.

IT'S ABOUT TIME THINGS CHANGED

Our personal lives have a direct impact on our work lives with regards to our productivity, performance, development, and engagement. Regardless of the degree we earned, our field, or the quantity of jobs we will have, one-third of our lives will be spent at work. Numerous aspects related to our jobs will become interlaced with our personal lives: our company, the culture, benefits, development programs, opportunities, bosses, and coworkers. Every day there are people who return to work only days after losing a loved one, who use their allotted time off for their chemotherapy sessions or post-surgery treatments, and who attend therapy sessions following their work shifts.[40]

Today—especially with the capabilities to work from home on the weekends and constant connectivity—the line drawn to distinguish and establish work-life balance has turned into invisible ink. With blurred boundaries between our work and home lives being an inevitable part of our lives, it can often feel like we can never catch our breath. In our professions, challenges can arise such as deciding whether or not to accept a promotion that requires relocation or reporting a colleague who falsified company documents.

It is just as difficult to leave our personal situations at the threshold of our homes as it is to leave all our work-related stressors at the office. The American Institute of Stress has discovered that stress directly related to either personal or professional situations causes around one million workers to be absent from work every day and costs over one trillion dollars per year in lost productivity. Being under stress and enduring pain for prolonged periods of time can lead to burnout—the tipping point of all-encompassing exhaustion where you become unable to work at all, out of sync, and

---

40 Andrew Naber, "One Third of Your Life Is Spent at Work," *Gettysburg College News*, May 16, 2020.

mentally disengaged. Burnout can also spark the onset of serious mental health issues.[41]

Additionally, over 60 percent of employees surveyed by the Anxiety and Depression Association of America stated they didn't feel comfortable talking with their manager or employer about the stress they're burdened with for the primary reason that they don't feel like their employer will be able to offer any form of support.[42]

If current distress levels do not change or continue to go unnoticed, the prediction is that over a quarter of employees worldwide will be at risk of burning out in the next twelve months. Stress, suffering, grief, depression, trauma, and physiological health problems can negatively affect businesses due to absenteeism, loss of productivity, and increased medical costs due to employee benefits. These problems can also interfere with the employees' abilities to complete physical job tasks and daily functioning, reducing their overall cognitive performance. Relationships and team dynamics can also experience tension and a lack of communication. [43]

Ultimately, the overall engagement, recruitment, and retention of employees will start trending downward.

---

41 "42 Worrying Workplace Stress Statistics," The American Institute of Stress, September 25, 2019; Melinda Smith, Jeanne Segal, and Lawrence Robinson, "Burnout Prevention and Treatment," HelpGuide, October 2019.

42 "Highlights: Workplace Stress & Anxiety Disorders Survey," Anxiety and Depression Association of America, accessed on February 12, 2020.

43 Mason Steveson, "Employee Burnout Statistics You Need to Know," HR Exchange Network, January 16, 2020.

* * *

The same building block lessons and continuous growth mindset can also transcend throughout our work and personal lives. Whether you're faced with a roadblock on your life's journey, collaborating on a project, or being promoted to a more senior role, gaining new perspectives grants you a better understanding of your work, role, coworkers, organization, or task at hand and lets you embrace innovative ideas. Compassion—both at home and in the workplace—fosters environments filled with human connection, loyalty, active listening, selflessness, and kindness. Gratitude helps us recognize how the positive things in our lives like joyful moments, celebrations, appreciation, recognition, and success at work are the results of the collaborative and uplifting efforts of a group of people.

One of the most beautiful attributes of the building blocks is their seamless ability to enable us to prevail over our challenges, work through uncertainty, and rejoice over our success, accomplishments, and overall self-worth—in both the home and the office cubicle. In the next few sections, I will share how the building blocks can be applicable for both employees and leaders to transform themselves and others while enhancing the company's talent life cycle of hiring, engaging, developing, and retaining.

EMPLOYEES: FROM LOOKING "EXCEPTIONAL ON PAPER" TO OWNING THEIR STORY

Our experiences are unique to our life's journey, teaching us valuable skills, instilling the building blocks and continuous growth lifestyle, and revealing noteworthy aspects about ourselves along the way. Much of the building blocks and continuous growth we discover at our lowest of lows are learned through experience. Furthermore, the life hurdles that teach us the building blocks are unconventional to put on a résumé or mention in an interview, but they do indeed show important skills you learn in real life that are remarkably applicable in the workplace.

It has always intrigued me how our challenges are not typically included on a résumé. On countless occasions throughout interviews, networking events, and job shadowing excursions, business professionals tend to rotate between similar "Tell me about yourself," situational, or behavioral questions.

"Tell me about a time when you handled a difficult conversation regarding a sensitive matter."

"Share a time when you had to rely on written communication to get your ideas across."

"Provide an example of when you worked through a conflict while collaborating with a team. "

I certainly had more than one answer to these interviewing questions based off of my academics, leadership positions, and working experiences, yet I personally feel that overcoming my family's derailment with a rare cancer taught me significantly more than anything else. On a few occasions during networking opportunities and interviews, I have briefly explained the lessons that I acquired during my dad's battle with cancer:

My family's life hurdle taught me how to embrace adaptability as I navigated uncharted waters and had uncomfortable conversations with my teachers, guidance counselor, and friends about my dad's cancer.

Writing a children's book opened a door for me to be vulnerable and transparent with my dad about my true thoughts and feelings about our unexpected circumstance. Furthermore, as I reflected upon my experiences, it allowed me to practice gratitude because I recognized how this challenge allowed me to gain appreciation for all the hills and valleys I traversed this far in my life to be here in this moment.

Resiliency gave me all the strength I needed to help my lacrosse team prevail in winning a match that, for the first half, left me bloody, bruised, and feeling utterly defeated.

Upon replying to their questions, the interviewers were profoundly impressed that I acquired these desirable qualities and skills necessary for the workplace and leadership roles during my family's struggles.

On an ordinary résumé, you often do not include moments or aspects of your life such as beating cancer, growing up in an abusive or violent environment, or staying sober for three consecutive years. Yet, our circumstances that we overcome shape us into the person we are today, just as equally if not more than a leadership position, an after-school volunteer program, or earning top honors.

It's important to recognize that your setbacks mold you into your authentic self and instill skills within you that can only be acquired through immersive experiences and positive reinforcement, which can prepare you for your profession. Some people may not feel comfortable sharing their experiences during an interview or until they establish a strong sense of trust. Personally, I found an indirect way to put my theory into action through—once again—writing.

In the early stages of my Human Resources career, I became interested in how the building blocks and continuous growth mindset can be vital capabilities that all employees should embrace. I ended up writing an article in my own time about how the building block lessons are the missing puzzle pieces in today's leadership. After writing this piece and sharing it with my manager at the time, they asked if my article could be distributed to a few other managers in Human Resources. I thought that would be a great idea, never expecting my insights to weave their way throughout the company, all the way to the executive suite.

One morning, I opened Outlook to find an email from a Vice President of a sector of the company for which I had not yet encountered. In the email, they shared that after reading my article, they were inspired and moved to find opportunities to embrace several of the building blocks and the continuous growth mindset within their role as a leader and on the teams they support. We scheduled a meeting so they could learn more about my insights on the topic and how both themselves and their team could embody these building blocks and mindset.

"What are ways we can practice employee self-care in the workplace?"

"How can I inspire my teams to simultaneously embrace resiliency and adaptability when working on extensive yet time-sensitive projects?"

"Are there any resources available to encourage my individual contributors to express more compassion toward one another as they acquire each other's unique perspectives on various initiatives?"

Devoting time to answering the VP's powerful questions and recommending some call to action items that would gradually implement these ideas over time was a humbling and rewarding experience. Companies cannot just simply say that human capital is their most vital asset—they must put their beliefs into ongoing motion. They need to incorporate, emphasize, and reinforce the building blocks and continuous growth mindset to make life's moments and challenges worthwhile, meaningful, and empowering. It is a process that requires the engagement of all the employees to co-create a stellar culture that other organizations cannot copy, built upon the transformative stories of trials and triumphs.

I advise that we should embrace and capitalize upon the skills, capabilities, and lessons learned from our challenges in our profession. Relating to your experiences and sharing *your* story can allow you to bridge meaningful, personal connections throughout your life, perhaps even landing you an offer for your dream job.

LEADERS AND MANAGERS: LEVERAGING ABILITIES TO LISTEN, SHARE, AND INSPIRE

If you were to research the top traits a company looks for in rising leaders, change-makers, and future CEOs, all eight building blocks and the continuous growth mindset would make the list. It takes years for high-level leaders or executives to fully embody some of these building block capabilities; some might retire never acquiring the building blocks and continuous growth mindset.

It doesn't matter what title of leadership you hold—be it an individual contributor, project manager, team leader, manager, director, or top executive—*everyone* is a leader and all leaders must care about and invest in their peers and employees. Employees want their managers to care about what is going in their lives and to be supportive on both personal and professional levels. They are not just employees—they are people too.

Employees often leave workplaces because of poor leadership. If managers and leaders truly care about what's going on beyond office hours in their employees' lives, it will grant them opportunities to gain perspective on their employees' lives, empower them to grow, share their experiences, find what motivates them, and help them solve real issues that are difficult to leave behind at home.

Leaders should commit to engaging with each employee on a personal level through productive one-on-one sessions to check in on how they are doing personally and see if they need assistance from a professional or personal standpoint. They need to ask their employees, teammates, and colleagues what makes them get out of bed in the morning, how has their story unfolded up to this moment, and what they envision for themselves in the upcoming weeks, months, and years.

Leaders should demonstrate compassion for their employees to strengthen relationships, embrace their employees' authenticity, and devote quality time for listening to employees express their feelings and concerns. This compassion will allow them to better meet the needs of those they oversee and gain perspectives on their employees' work-life situation.

Sharing experiences should not be reserved only for employees; leaders, too, at all levels within organizations, need to set an example by sharing their personal challenges and modeling the building blocks and continuous growth mindset. Employees want to feel inspired and motivated. Hearing their leaders' stories, struggles, and experiences would give them inspiration.

In many organizations, leaders are often viewed as singular individuals who are meant to be perfect, flawless, and rigid. Any sign or suspicion of weakness would mean they are unfit for their roles. A common perception among leaders—specifically those who are in the business realm—is they may lose their leadership credibility for showing their humanity. Having leaders be open to sharing their experiences requires overcoming the gendered stereotypes and societal norms of how vulnerable a person should be. Women are often told they are too emotional, meanwhile it is considered socially unacceptable for men to openly share how they are feeling. Men are expected to always be the leader and uphold the rigid, traditional ideals of masculinity that are so deeply rooted in capitalism.

Leaders struggle to break down these barriers because they are afraid to be human, and they believe they cannot fully express their genuine feelings and thoughts. I have participated in several executive meetings that are meant to be discussion-driven so everyone can have moments to share experiences, opinions, and thoughts. However, when the presenter turns the discussion over to the executives, none of them wanted to speak. I could tell from their mannerisms they were nervous, anxious, and even scared to express themselves.

In one of those meetings, the silence was so incredibly awkward that at one point I, a mere college student, decided to voice my perspective and insights in front of ten executives. Through these meetings, I learned by observation that I want to be a leader who's comfortable engaging in discussions, whether the topic be about employee recognition, engagement, or talent management.

A true, effective leader acquires a novel perspective when viewing all the ups and downs of their own experiences to understand those of their employees. A leader who can do that would be inspirational and genuine, would continually strive to reinforce trust, and would embrace the inclusion of all employees. One of my former managers exemplified these astonishing qualities. They prioritized having hour-long, one-on-one meetings that dived into deep reflection about our experiences, insights, and aspirations. During these talks, my manager wanted to leverage my perspective by requesting genuine feedback about how they can better support my development and improve as a manager.

In one of our earlier meetings, my manager asked, "How did Human Resources become your passion?"

As we walked through Downtown Pittsburgh along the Allegheny River, I spoke transparently with my manager, revealing the true reason why I found human resources to be my professional passion. I told them how my dad worked in Human Resources for over thirty years and each day he came home with his passion and appreciation for his work evident in his brimming smile. Then, I briefly retold the story about my dad's battle with cancer and how I had initially feared my dad would not be able to return to work again.

Upon learning the news regarding my family's derailment, I spent several days pondering my dad's admiration of his career and reflecting on how I wanted a career path that enabled me to leverage my love for learning and development. I realized that Human Resources is essentially about managing employees by hiring, developing, engaging, and retaining them, and became committed to pursuing this career path, simultaneously carrying out my dad's legacy.

Once I shared this with my manager, they felt honored that I vulnerably shared my personal connection to Human Resources.

"It truly makes sense now why you're committed to this profession," my manager replied wholeheartedly.

Recognizing how Human Resources was a true passion of mine, my manager invited me to as many meetings, training programs, and networking opportunities as they could.

A few weeks after this conversation, I walked onto my floor to find my manager sitting at their desk, looking defeated and exhausted.

I barely had a chance to set my backpack down on my desk and log into my laptop when they asked me, "Spontaneous coffee run?"

"Sounds good," I replied as we headed down to the bustling streets of Pittsburgh's morning rush hour.

While waiting in line for our lattes, I thought my manager wanted to have another productive brainstorming session. However, little did I know my manager really needed my reassurance and support. They transparently admitted they were anxious because their father was having surgery today. Their parents lived out of state, so they were not able to physically be there to support their dad.

"I knew you would understand how I am feeling," my manager stated to me. "It's good to have someone like you on my team who knows what's going on; we can definitely support each other."

My manager was so incredibly moved by my personal experiences, insights, and stories that they shared what was going on in their mind and burdening their heart; this, in turn, created a psychologically safe environment in which to work and prioritized authentic experiences and intrinsic qualities rather than external characteristics. This environment allowed us to embrace and learn from our experiences, which created a stronger foundation of confidence and reassurance among our team, sparked the onsets of new projects, discussions, and initiatives, and provided further opportunities to advance our development.

Our personal challenges can positively transform our professional experiences as well as provide opportunities for employees and leaders as we continually progress within an organization. Through the continuous reinforcement of the building blocks and the growth mindset, employees will find fulfillment in their lives and professions, and leaders and managers will be able to keep their employees happy, retained, and engaged. Having a healthy, vibrant, and transparent company culture requires the endorsement of all leaders.

The commitment that employees make to actively integrate their stories in staff meetings, interactive sessions, and one-on-one meetings can forge opportunities to capitalize and own their challenges. By sharing their stories, they can learn to view their challenges as part of their journey and greater life purpose. Finding all the good, possibilities, and teachings that can emerge from our temporary setbacks and applying it through various facets of our lives both personally and professionally can begin with one spark—one employee—to become the living proof that we can thrive through and beyond life's moments both at home and in the office.

PART IV

OUT OF THE DARKNESS AND INTO THE BEYOND

CHAPTER 16

NEW BEGINNINGS, BARRIERS, AND BRIDGES

Overcoming my dad's cancer made my already satisfying life story more compelling, meaningful, and purposeful. My ordinary life of fifteen years transformed into an extraordinary adventure of self-discovery and continuous growth. My family went from being engulfed in uncertainty to experiencing life to the fullest. I no longer simply *lived* my life; I became committed to thrive in all the valleys and hilltops of my life's mountainous landscape. Like archaeologists uncovering artifacts and fossils of past civilizations, during my dad's confrontation with olfactory neuroblastoma cancer, the building block concepts revealed themselves to me. They became ingrained in me, coming into the spotlight of my life through my intentions, passions, and purpose once I swept away the dust and darkness.

Since the initial onset of my family's derailment, I felt certain my whole life was still ahead of me with greater and better things in the distance; my life was not meant to be stagnant.

I believed this challenge crossed my path because it had a purpose: to teach me the building blocks to reveal what I am truly capable of and to prove to myself this challenge would prepare me to seize all future endeavors and prevail in forthcoming obstacles. Little did I know my intuition and theory would manifest themselves, transforming my undergraduate career and Jesuit education at John Carroll University into a remarkable experience—perhaps the best four years I could have ever asked for.

* * *

In late August 2015, after graduating from high school, I left the familiar borders of Pittsburgh in which I lived for eighteen years to make the three-hour trek to the east side of Downtown Cleveland. Along with my shower caddy, a giant pile of textbooks, and my favorite childhood white, stuffed-animal dog, I brought along the lessons of the building blocks, my academic drive, and my enthusiasm as I dove into organizations, clubs, and leadership roles.

Attending John Carroll University was the first time I was away from home for more than a week. With nervous butterflies in my stomach, it was hard to say "see you soon" to my parents after enduring the battle with cancer. Yet, we all knew I was ready for another new adventure of my own.

When I started my freshman year, I decided to step outside my comfort zone and register for sorority recruitment to learn about the five chapters on campus and hopefully find a chapter to join. I enjoyed all the conversations I had with all the chapters, but there was one chapter in particularly that my heart subconsciously gravitated toward: Kappa Delta.

When I chatted with the Kappa Delta women during the rounds, I felt accepted, cherished, valued and truly me; they saw my potential and inner beauty emerge through our conversations. It was the only chapter with which I conveyed my dad's cancer story, my aspiration to write a book someday, and my passion for human resources. It was the only chapter that felt like home.

I had found where I belonged, surrounded by fifty sisters.

Within Kappa Delta, I also had a family: Nina, Anna, and Lilian—Big, Little, and Grand-Little—the best family and sisters I could have ever been blessed with and who inspire me to always move forward to seize my potential.

My four years at John Carroll University presented me with countless friendships that filled my life with amazing people. The love, compassion, and humility my friends and sorority sisters showed me was immeasurable. They always knew when I needed to laugh, have a night out, a shoulder to cry on, or another cup of coffee. All of them deeply cared about my happiness and success just as much or more than I did; they saw a whole life ahead of me full of endless possibilities.

In addition to embracing new friendships and relationships, attending one of the twenty-eight Jesuit Universities in the United States renewed my spirituality and faith. This led me closer to my precious relationship with God, Jesus, and all the saints who reign above me. A Jesuit education is deeply rooted in valuable teachings such as striving for excellence in learning, becoming adaptable and open to growth, finding God in all things, and serving the faith that does justice.

Growing spiritually expanded my definition of gratitude to more than being simply thankful; I recognized the power of prayer, the devotion to sharing the good news, and the emphasis on living the life God has specifically chosen for me were all gifts of gratitude. Also, as a Carroll Faith Community leader, I started holding healthy and engaging discussions with my group about facing the stressors in our lives by sharing the story about my dad's battle with cancer.

As a student at John Carroll University, I readily used and expanded upon my authenticity and compassion. I discovered an inner peace and appreciation for my authentic self by volunteering, attending mass at 9:00 p.m., and having daily conversations with fellow students and faculty. Furthermore, practicing gratitude and my faith became a part of my self-care routine. Quite often, I would make my way to our campus chapel, St. Francis, before the sun would rise. I would sit up front by the altar to enjoy the silence and presence of God. In those moments, I never felt alone, for I was surrounded by infinite love that warmed my heart, which calmed me down and energized my soul to work toward my purpose.

Beyond my spiritual growth, I began taking classes specifically designed for my major in the spring semester of my sophomore year. My degree in Human Resources and Management from the Boler College of Business was more than something engraved on a piece of fancy paper: it was a part of my genuine identity and my passion. I loved learning, studying, and pursuing Human Resources because it gave me opportunities to be proud of myself, revealed my strengths and weaknesses, and filled my heart with joy and happiness. Pursuing a degree in Human Resources also leveraged the building blocks within me that became vital to seizing upcoming professional opportunities.

Some of my opportunities to leverage the building blocks came through my college leadership roles and extracurricular activities. I learned how to become an effective leader and serve my community. Through my sorority life experience, I discovered I valued the interactions I had with the other sororities and fraternities, embracing the idea of being a part of a larger community beyond my own sorority chapter. Within this passion, I placed my heart, soul, and energy toward serving the Fraternity & Sorority Life Community as a Recruitment Counselor and VP of Recruitment & Membership.

In addition to the two Greek life positions, I held other positions as Business & Finance Co-Editor of *The Carroll News,* scorekeeper for the Intramural & Recreation Department, and a Carroll Faith Community Leader for Campus Ministry. By holding these leadership roles, I developed my true voice, which granted me opportunities to empower and inspire others to embrace new perspectives or seize various moments, to ensure intramural teams demonstrated good sportsmanship, and to motivate sorority women to work through new changes in our recruitment season.

Using my voice to inspire others required me to be both transparent and vulnerable in my diverse leadership roles across the organizations, putting these building blocks into action. Furthermore, I made conscious and continual efforts to illustrate to my team, group, and chapters that making progressive change forward and overcoming adversities would help us all grow as a community.

* * *

With a strong sisterhood, a rekindled faith, a fantastic major, and exceptional leadership opportunities that were brought forth to me, I had an amazing four years at John Carroll University. However, my time on campus did not fully materialize without experiencing countless stressors related to intense coursework, time management skills, and prioritizing all my activities and jobs. There were setbacks I encountered that shook the very core of my being, made me question everything I know about my life, and reinforced the building blocks I had previously learned. These setbacks reminded me that what I would continually learn during my four years at university would transcend beyond the lecture halls and classrooms.

During my sophomore year, my days started at 5:45 a.m. with a run around the campus or a workout session at the University Recreation Center before my classes started at 8:00 a.m. Next, I attended all my classes, followed by regular homework or study sessions at the library, working at my part-time job, being an active member of five different organizations, and spending time with my sorority sisters and close friends. I was fortunate if I could squeeze in time to eat two meals a day and get back to my dorm at night so I could at least get a good seven hours of sleep. I strove to accomplish it all and aimed higher than what was already considered to be exceptional.

For most college students, some challenges that can manifest include adjusting to living independently, meeting the scores of professors' expectations, and dealing with the overwhelming pressure to attend parties, stay up until dawn, or skip class. For me, the first setback I stumbled upon during my collegiate experience was quite different.

It was mid-November with about five weeks left in the fall semester. For five nights in a row, I hardly got any sleep because I had difficulty breathing through my nose. My complexion turned paler than normal, my hands were stone cold and clammy, and the persistent discomfort in my chest suffocated me. A few of my sisters and friends started to worry that I had more than a short-lived cold and advised me to take it easy and check in with my parents. At the end of that week of pain, on Saturday afternoon my mom and dad video called me to catch up from the previous week.

With one glance at me and without any hesitation, my mom said, "Pack your bag and email your professors because your dad is driving up to bring your home tomorrow morning. Something isn't right."

By Monday afternoon, after an entire morning spent getting x-rayed and examined by medical professionals, the tests revealed that my entire right lung was filled with mucus. I was diagnosed with pneumonia. Bedridden for three weeks and too weak to complete any assignments, I had boundless time to pause, reevaluate, and reflect upon the past several weeks with a different perspective, which led to the discovery of how this all happened.

At John Carroll, I was constantly on the move and my to-do lists kept getting longer. I was running to and from, studying for exams, attending sorority meetings, working a four-hour shift, and staying out late with friends. I became exhausted and drained after putting 110 percent into every moment of every day; as a result, I became burnt out within the first three semesters of college.

I embodied resiliency during my case of pneumonia. I did not want to let this illness impede the rest of my plans for college. I realized that the excessive stress—even if most of it was positively associated with my collegiate experience—resulted in mental and physical exhaustion, the reduction of self-care, and the downfall of my overall health. Through a deep reflection, I realized I was stretching myself too thin by participating in a number of organizations that were not emphatically contributing to my overall development and life moments.

From then on, I prioritized placing my focus and energy on my coursework, activities, and experiences that aligned with my interests and passions. I chose to solely engage in activities that propelled me to be my authentic self. I decided to create a schedule that promoted self-care—one that allotted free time, granted me flexibility, and allowed me to enjoy and soak in the remainder of my college years.

With an updated game plan and mindset, I regained my energy and motivation to complete the fall semester with a strong finish while narrowing down my extracurricular activities to those that would better serve me on individual and professional levels. I averted my attention toward finding all the possible means I could to incorporate the building blocks and continuous growth mindset into all aspects of my undergrad experience and thrive beyond this setback.

CHAPTER 17

FROM NOWHERE TO EVERYWHERE

Having pneumonia was physically painful, yet I am grateful that being bedridden for three weeks forced me to think about my true aspirations, interests, and passions. I vulnerably admitted to myself that trying to do everything and be *the best* was only causing me to suffer on all levels of my well-being. I assessed how I felt physically, mentally, and emotionally so I could figure out what I could do to change to better my life. I acknowledged I needed to strike a balance between achieving an operating level that was *my* best and enjoying my undergrad career.

With this new intention set, I thoroughly enjoyed the rest of my collegiate experience until another obstacle derailed me off my well-paved path. The additional setback I endured occurred toward the halfway point of my last fall semester. I took only twelve credits and closed out my term in a few of my leadership positions. All of a sudden, with a swish and a flick from a wand, I had all this free time—more than I ever had before in my life. Other than finishing out the last eight classes of my undergrad and completing my senior capstone project in the spring, I did not have much to do and didn't feel like I had much of a purpose left on campus.

At the end of October, I noticed I had trouble getting adequate rest. For a few nights in a row, my heart would race exponentially, my mind would not stop thinking, and my body felt restless. I felt the need to be productive and do something . . . anything! On Halloween, I experienced extreme chest pain for over twelve hours and could barely breathe. As soon as our University Health Center opened the next morning, I went in to see one of the nurses. After describing my lasting symptoms, they instructed me to go to the Emergency Room.

On my way to the hospital, I called my parents to admit to them how I had been feeling and I was headed to the Cleveland Clinic Emergency Room. At the hospital, the medical professionals asked me a never-ending stream of questions about my past and current circumstances, marking off items and taking notes on a clipboard while simultaneously checking my pulse.

Hours later, I walked out of the Emergency Room with a diagnosis of an intense panic attack.

Even more concerning, they determined I experienced persistent, elevated anxiety levels and illustrated some of the early-onset symptoms of both an anxiety disorder and post-traumatic stress disorder (PTSD).

For six months following this diagnosis, I was not my authentic self; I was someone completely and utterly different. During that time, I found it exceedingly difficult to be happy, to be loved, and to find a reason—*any reason*—to stay in the present because I relentlessly questioned my existence, life, and purpose. Instead of my mind being filled with knowledge from my Human Resources textbooks, excitement for upcoming events with my best friends and sisters, and anticipation to enter the workplace immediately after graduation, self-destructive thoughts and feelings tormented me every waking hour.

I felt like I was collapsing inward.

It was as if everything I had ever worked for washed away with the frequent tears that cascaded down my face. I was afraid and lost in my own life. I felt corrupted by this foreign force that took over all control of my thoughts, emotions, and perceptions of myself, just like how Harry Potter felt in *The Order of the Phoenix* when Voldemort controlled his mind. It affected my sleep, social interactions, appetite, and in-class participation.

My parents struggled to comprehend why my mental and emotional well-being was in disarray. We all wanted what was best for me. All three of us knew I needed to seek some guidance and help; however, we all agreed I should not delay my graduation, especially with only four classes standing between me and my diploma.

At the start of the spring semester of my senior year, I ultimately decided to complete my last semester partially remote, dividing my time between campus and home. Sharing this news to a few of my close friends and faculty about my situation was excruciating; it made my whole body quiver. Knowing I wouldn't be able to make amazing memories during my last semester and enjoy the company of my friends was a painful reality, yet it was the path I chose to walk so I could simultaneously complete my degree and recover.

* * *

While putting on a happy face in utter chaos, I tried to make an effort in all my classes, participate in any meetings or events my organizations planned, and attend regular sessions with counselors, therapists, a chiropractor, and a health and wellness expert. I continued to work hard at school and in my extracurricular activities, yet the fulfilling, authentic, and passionate pieces were missing. I still felt terrible inside.

Having conversations with friends, family, professors, advisers, and counselors eased my discomfort temporarily. With my keen memory, I replayed these conversations in my mind and wrote them down safely in a journal as a part of the healing process from the trauma I experienced. Yet, they all worried about me and did not know how to truly assist me. They wondered what had happened to my enthusiasm, passion, self-love, interests, strong academics, and love for life itself that once made me radiant. I had trouble communicating what was going on in my mind. I was at a loss for words when trying to decrypt why I was suddenly feeling this way. I felt helpless, sick, and ashamed. I did not know what to do or how to move beyond the anxiety and depression that consumed my body, mind, and soul.

It took me until the second week of May—the start of finals week—for the hazy fog surrounding me to begin to clear so the sunlight could shine in. In the midst of preparing for my senior capstone presentation the next morning about my talent life cycle and management theory, I made a shocking realization that finally turned on all the light bulbs in my head: all the suggestions, recommendations, and words of encouragement my support systems shared with me were relating back to the building blocks and the continuous growth mindset. As I processed this realization, I recalled how one of my professors reminded me to be resilient, Anna showed me compassion, and Jason reinforced within me the authenticity and self-care building blocks.

Knowing the burden I was carrying, one of my Business College professors shared an insight with me:

"I admire your resilience, commitment, and passion during your time at John Carroll, just as much as you said I have inspired you during my lectures. It has been a great joy to watch you surmount every expectation, both personal and professional. I am grateful for that and I know that you have a whole life ahead of you of inspiring others!"

That professor reminded me of the importance of resiliency and that I still had the power to be resilient despite my struggle with my mental health.

During dinner in the cafeteria or evening chats with my little in my sorority, Anna, she would demonstrate true compassion toward me:

"I'm not giving up the idea that you are going to prevail over your setbacks, Nicole. You are too strong to give up; believe in and love yourself as much as I do. Just keep moving forward!"

Anna's encouragement reminded me of the power of being compassionate toward myself during these trying times.

Through several text conversations and phone calls, Jason reassured me that I am not the only one who has ever questioned whether or not they have a purpose.

"You should be proud of yourself and celebrate the progress you have made, because I certainly am! You have a purpose, Nicole—just let your passions take you there. I can't wait to see what you do next!"

Jason's encouragement illustrated the importance of recognizing all of the things I've accomplished so far as part of my self-care and authentic self.

I was resilient when running a successful Sorority Recruitment Weekend. I capitalized on the gratitude, the power of prayer, and blessings deeply rooted in my spirituality and the Jesuit teachings. I allowed my authenticity to radiate through my leadership roles and my academic assignments. However, being burdened by anxiety and PTSD caused a landslide of fear and distress that buried these qualities, making it challenging for me to reinforce and equip them easily from my toolkit.

I had the opposite problem than I had my sophomore year; rather than being constantly on the go, I had nowhere to go and felt completely stagnant. I had started to let the anxiety and PTSD define the rest of my life. I was going down the black hole of the hardwired negativity mindset that is typically our default setting when confronted with obstacles.

I became my own worst and harshest critic, doubting everything in my life and all I had accomplished.

My family, friends, sorority sisters, and professors did not think for a single second that I would surrender to my fears and stressors; they knew I would rise above and beyond them. They all knew I had these building blocks within me and witnessed how I have utilized them before in previous circumstances beyond my dad's battle with cancer.

The supportive people in my life reminded me of how far I have come and how much is ahead of me. They believed in my capabilities more than I believed in myself. They knew I would prevail, and they could visualize my transformation . . . my beyond . . . my purpose. Yet, *I* had to be the one to affirm those statements and set them into motion to turn the page of my life's story to reveal the title of the next chapter.

* * *

Overcoming burnout and managing my anxiety and PTSD emphasized how I am constantly learning and developing, even if I am not enrolled as a student at a university anymore. I am a work in progress and live for learning more about myself, my capabilities, and my true intentions. With each step forward I move closer to my goals, passions, and mission. Overcoming those challenges taught me that I have no excuse to ever doubt my worth or hide my genuine self. I should accept who I am, be proud of myself, and celebrate the achievements I have accomplished thus far, as well as those that are yet to come.

The two derailments I endured during my undergrad experience fortified the importance of the building blocks and continuously growing; I learned they aren't tools meant to collect dust on an unreachable shelf. Rather, they are important to always keep at hand to help spark my internal drive and propel me forward to seize all of the opportunities that await me in the days, weeks, months, and years to come.

During my collegiate experience, the building blocks and growth mindset transformed those four years into the best I could have ever hoped for. With this mindset, my journey at John Carroll University led me to flourish in my academics, extracurricular and professional positions, spirituality, and relationships.

These capabilities radiated through my exams, senior capstone project, presentations, and conversations with fellow classmates and professors. I certainly didn't go unnoticed—toward the end of my senior year, while overcoming my anxiety and PTSD and struggling to put effort into my coursework, the faculty of the Boler College of Business recognized me as the "Outstanding Senior in Human Resources and Management" and awarded me with Magma Cum Laude Honors during graduation.

All those experiences in college made me more optimistic, reaffirmed my abilities, and reassured me that I have a wonderful life journey ahead of me. I knew I was prepared for life as an adult and a working professional. I give quite a bit of credit to the building blocks and the continuous growth mindset; they allow me to make unceasing, onward, and affirmative progress throughout both trying and triumphant times in my life. If it wasn't for those tools, I wouldn't have excelled in my academics at a highly-rated private university, leveraged my leadership skills in several professional and extracurricular activities, and had fantastic friends who always believed in my capabilities now and in the future.

In the current moment, the continuous growth mindset sparks my drive to seize future opportunities, fulfill my true potential, and become readily equipped to brave more hurdles. The final part of preparing for the rest of my journey is to make a clear and unequivocal promise to myself that I am absolutely committed to the journey that lies beyond for me to discover, achieve, and cherish.

My hope is for you, as the reader, to take the stories of how the building blocks and continuous growth mindset pulled me beyond my college challenges and use them as tools to improve your own life. They will truly allow you heal, love, thrive, discover, enjoy, and live your journey. Ever-evolving growth throughout your life is necessary—greater plans are in store for us that have yet to be unveiled, and you need to trust the way your journey is unfolding.

CHAPTER 18

A REFLECTION

In those six long months of my spring semester of my senior year, I stayed resilient and placed all the strength I could muster into truly enjoying the remaining threads of my college experience: Greek Week, my sorority formal, and graduation. Happiness and joy still did not come easily; after hitting rock bottom, I knew it would be an uphill battle to gradually make my way back up the mountain and witness my beyond in the horizon. It would require patience and persistence to have the courage to transcend the darkness that had blanketed me.

Yet, eventually all that changed, making the darkness, depression, distress, and dismay a permanent memory of the past.

Upon graduating from John Carroll University in May 2019, I returned to Pittsburgh for a job opportunity located downtown. Although I was thrilled and fortunate to have a professional job to dive into right out of college, I was still trying to regain my strength and determination after battling with anxiety, PTSD, depression, and self-confidence. During this time, I also struggled to realize my college days were over and process the news of a close family member's cancer diagnosis. I soul searched, trying to get back on my life's path, and set my navigation system to drive toward my purpose that friends, family, professors, and colleagues saw for me.

However, something was obstructing my view.

JUNE 14, 2019

The clock struck five o'clock on a Friday evening in June, just as I finished sending an email. I closed my laptop, packed my bag, and bounded toward the main floor of my office's skyscraper building. Typically, I would have headed down another flight of stairs to catch the next available train back home. However, my heart and soul had other intentions that evening; I experienced this sudden yearning to wander, feel free, and explore—to go see what lies further ahead.

Since I had returned from college, I had not had a chance to roam the familiar Pittsburgh streets that were my home and a part of me. I made the split-second decision to head out through the main entrance of my work building. The moment I made it out of the revolving glass doors of my work building, I found myself running—in wedges and a dress, mind you.

I ran with pure joy and anticipation, feeling like I was returning to my authentic self after those six painful months of depression. I dodged people heading to their bus or train, past those waiting to get up onto rooftop bars for happy hour and waved to those who recognized me at local shops and hotels. I was not running away from my past, my fears, or stressors. I was running toward something, somewhere. From Steel Plaza past the brick-laid Market Square lined with bustling restaurants and string-lights illuminating the square, I ran all the way to Fifth Avenue Place on the other side of central downtown, soaking in the most gorgeous evening I could have could ask for.

Once I arrived at Fifth Avenue Place, I stopped running and decided to casually stroll toward Point State Park, located where the Allegheny and Monongahela rivers merge into the Ohio River. On the walk over to Point, there were hardly any other human beings in sight.

I walked around the park's fountain as if I was admiring a world-renowned sculpture, fine water droplets fluttering around me. Halfway around the fountain I made a detour and walked to the edge of the cemented steps of the park, sensing the entire city of Pittsburgh bustling behind me.

Although I have lived my whole life in Pittsburgh, I had never witnessed this particular view in person before. Standing at the edge, I saw the Ohio River flowing endlessly onward, stretching for miles and miles. This water would eventually end up in the Mississippi River, move gradually south all the way into the Gulf of Mexico, and get carried away in relentless currents and waves in the oceans that span the globe.

After staring off into the distance, I glanced downward, and what I saw was beautiful. The three rivers in Pittsburgh are known for being a bit murky and opaque; however, at that pivotal moment, I could see my reflection as clear as it would appear in a mirror. I saw myself—both the woman I am now, and the woman I am becoming.

Seeing my reflection prompted me to look back on my life, sparking the onset of vivid flashbacks. I revisited the day I graduated Magma Cum Laude from John Carroll University, the twelve weeks of my Talent Management internship alongside the most incredible professionals, the weekend I joined my home away from home in Kappa Delta, the night I went to my Senior Prom alongside eleven girls that are still some of my closest friends, the last lacrosse game I ever played and wore the number twenty proudly, and the morning I saw my dad run again nearly eight months after being diagnosed with cancer.

In that moment, I remembered all of the wonderful aspects of my life that emerged from my initial life-altering derailment. All those happy, fulfilling, and positive moments happened because I was able to overcome life's obstacles.

They were moments overflowing with new relationships, academic excellence, standing ovations, recognition, warm embraces, radiant smiles, and unconditional love.

Those moments are part of the beyond I was and always will be striving toward.

As I emerged from the looking glass, I discovered that the sun was beginning to set. Surrounding my reflection in the water were the magnificent colors of blood orange, pink, and yellow. I closed my eyes for a moment and slowly turned around. Reopening my eyes, I took in the wonderful view of Downtown Pittsburgh. I could see the entire city clearly with *nothing* in my way.

To my left, I saw the spotlights shining on PNC Park along the Allegheny and off to the right, the Gateway Clipper boat docking at Station Square on the Monongahela. Ahead of me were the looming skyscrapers in the Pittsburgh skyline, standing like giants. All around me, the night lights of Pittsburgh shone, radiating just as bright as they did the night I returned home from the hospital after my dad's surgery.

In that moment in the park, I felt alive.

I experienced a transformation.

My lungs were finally able to breathe again.

My heart no longer carried a heavy burden.

The negativity and harmful thoughts that had plagued my mind disappeared.

I felt infinite bliss and gratitude for the people, moments, events, conversations, and places that were a critical part of my life.

I loved and appreciated my life for what it had been, what it currently was, and what it would be.

As I stood admiring the Pittsburgh skyline, I thought about the building blocks I learned along the way that propelled me forward. I remembered all the people and events that I encountered along the way that reinforced my commitment to continually grow in my life. I did not find it difficult to look back on all the ups and downs of my life; instead, I gained appreciation and rejoiced after recognizing how far I have come to be in this present moment.

The past was behind me—all its fears, anxieties, negativity, doubt, and pressure. I had overcome so much, and I knew I could not go back. I could only move forward to continually grow, live, and thrive in my life. I had to read the next chapters of my story to discover my beyond.

I closed my eyes and as I took a deep breath, all the memories, capabilities, passions, and purposes flooded back into my life. With a smile on my sun-kissed face, I headed back toward the brilliance of Downtown Pittsburgh, toward all that awaited me in the rest of my life—finally reaching the light at the end at the tunnel.

AFTERWORD

FINAL THOUGHTS FROM THE BEYOND

AUTUMN 2020: SIXTEEN MONTHS LATER

As the transition of seasons brings vibrant colors of sunflower yellow, blood orange, and crimson red to the hilly woodlands of Western Pennsylvania, I continue to welcome change with a full embrace as if greeting a dear friend. Change and uncertainty are no strangers to me; in fact, they are perhaps one of my life's most unique and complex aspects.

With change comes new beginnings, new chapters, new relationships, and new opportunities. It teaches you lessons and gives you a magnifying glass and a pair of binoculars so you can see all the intricate aspects that make up who you currently are while looking out into the horizon to see the person you have the potential to become.

The next time change steers you in a different direction on your life's journey, remember it might be leading you there for a reason or it could be rerouting your journey to the next moment . . . to tomorrow . . . to your beyond.

When I reflect upon on my life—which is quite often—I'm still in awe at how all the ups and downs in my life are seamlessly connected. If I had traversed my challenges in a way that departed from the building blocks and continuous growth mindset, I might not have attended the same university, become a member of my sorority, majored in human resources, met some of the most amazing people in my life, or written the very book you are reading.

Little did I know, my dad's cancer, the sudden passing of loved ones, the x-ray showing my right lung filled with mucus, and my diagnosis of anxiety, panic attacks, and PTSD were only the beginning for me.

There were pure moments ahead of me in my life. Day in and day out, these moments come together to create the masterpiece I like to call my beyond.

There were, at times, moments of deep sadness, late night crying, stress, frustration, anger, heartache, and pain. Yet all of them were flushed away by the celebrations, laughter, love, accomplishments, runs, opportunities, jobs, coffee and dinner dates, long evening walks around campus, happy, uncontrollable tears, and dreams turned into reality.

Writing and publishing a book was a dream I left on the pillow for far too long, never imagining it would be a part of my beyond and lead me further toward my purpose and driving passions. The incredible book publishing opportunity came to me seven months after the reflective moment at Point State Park. I embarked on this book journey with a definite purpose: to become living proof that going beyond life's most uncertain, unprecedented, and difficult moments is a capability we all have.

By writing this book, I found the key that unlocked my true emotions, thoughts, and insights, moving me one step closer to my beyond. The very stories, lessons, pages, ink, and fragments embedded in this book are a part of my beyond.

I do not showcase these challenges as burdens weighing down my heart and shoulders, but as gifts brought into my life to teach lessons.

When I look back, I don't see a young woman suffocating under a pile of insecurities, grief, and worries; rather, I see her in full bloom as the sun's rays shower light from above.

Even in the most uncertain and unprecedented times, restoration, love, healing, infinite growth, laughter, happiness, and life are possible. Everything is possible.

* * *

As I pull up a chair to the front windows of my apartment with a cup of tea in hand, I take in the afterglow of the sunset. Its rays cast colorful, leaf-shaped shadows on the walls as time comes to a standstill.

Rather than fearing what tomorrow might bring or what challenges I might have to hurdle, I graciously and silently thank the sunset for what it brings:

A promise.

A sign.

A moment from my beyond.

ACKNOWLEDGMENTS

"We have a writer in the family."

I heard those words often from my dad's mother, my grandmother, to the point where they've been permanently inked in my mind. I never considered writing to be a chore, a mundane task, or a mere requirement of academia; it has been and will always be a definitive and affirmative part of my identity.

Writing became one of my hobbies around the age of six when I started to send handwritten letters to Nanny. We are still pen pals to this day.

It evolved into an interest in high school. I wrote entries in my journal about vacation trips, memorable days at school, and life milestones. Eventually, I entered writing contests and published articles in my school's news magazine.

Later on, writing became a passion when I discovered it could open doors for me, allowing me to speak volumes without uttering a word, unlocking my mind, expressing my genuine self, and flooding pages upon pages of journals with my deepest thoughts, feelings, moments, and intentions.

Now, writing is a way of life.

It got me through the happiest times and most tear-jerking moments of my life. It enabled me to work through my dad's battle with cancer and calm my nerves before my anxiety allowed any self-destructive thoughts to creep in. Most importantly, writing provided me with an unyielding sense of confidence, reassurance, and fulfillment.

Writing and publishing a book became a personal life goal. I wanted to share my story and experiences so I can inspire others through my writing.

And here we are.

As I reflect on my writing journey up to this very moment, I am infinitely thankful for the people who helped me throughout every chapter of this eye-opening, rigorous, vulnerable, and gratifying experience.

First and foremost, I would like to thank my family: Mom, Dad, and Corey. Thank you for seeing my potential even when I was blinded by my self-doubt. Your infinite love, support, compassion, and confidence fueled my drive to explore opportunities that would allow my passionate spirit to flourish. You all truly embody and live out the messages of this book. You are my inspirations and I love you always.

I am also grateful for everyone I interviewed for this book. Not only are your stories the foundation of *Beyond Life's Moments,* but our hours of meaningful conversation were by far the most moving and rewarding part of this entire journey. Thank you for your time, your energy, and your examples. You are true, inspiring heroes and your stories will live on in the beyond.

A *huge* thank you to my editors at New Degree Press—Karina Agbisit, Kristy Elam, and John Chancey—for their endless support, encouragement, and patience. I would also like to thank Professors Eric Koester and Brian Bies for guiding me through this long-awaited dream and turning it into a reality.

Finally, I'd like to thank everyone who preordered, donated, and helped spread the word about *Beyond Life's Moments* to help it gather momentum. From uplifting early praise to late night talks, I couldn't be more blessed to have an amazing group of people be a part of this unique journey!

My Author Community and Early Supporters: Steve and Beth Cherico, Nick D' Souza, Emily Nobers, Nina Carrino, Chris Adesso, Kayleigh Fuizzotti, Cortney Honeycutt, Courtney Emery, Deb Roos, Emily Mullen, Kassianna Politis, Tiffany Mosher, Doan Winkel, Courtney Chaplin, Brandon Posivak, Mary Kosanke, Zachary and Mackenzie Sivavec, Elizabeth Ivanecky, Lilian Lebednick, Tara Daly, Kate Foulke, Lucy Christoforetti, Nicole Sitler, Kaitlyn Grady, Madeline Smanik, Jason Wendel, Scott Allen, Angela Cramer, Kelsey O'Hara, Klaire Mathews, Duygu Qutubuddin, Krista Powell, Megan Frankenberger, Maria Getto, Colin Hendrickson, Anna Rastetter, Michelle Dunn, Ashley Johenning,

Eric Koester, Lauren Phillip, Vicki and Mark Aaron, Diane Noreen, Dana and Ben Glicksman, Tiffany Trunk, Marcia Dietz, Lori Schwerzler, Matt Rombalski, Corey Spindler, Kate Noreen, Marissa Haas, Emma Bevilacqua, Ashlen Sweeney, Jessica Cherico, Amanda Cherico, Amy Hannah, Linda Hannah, Ashley Mariuzza, Valentina Powell, Erin Brown, Wendy Stark, Toren Bakula, Haley Newlin, Alice and Ed Spindler, Nicole Mitchell, Michelle Little, Victor Cherico, Kennedy Young, Doug Brinkley, Jerry Tierney, Brittany Cole, Robin Janis, Jean Blachier, Madison Start, Michele MacKay, Denise Hitchens, J.B. and Audrey Wilcox, Mike Rajka, Nicole Folino, Hannah Gleichenhaus, Lisa Marking, Sean Cain, Caroline Brand, Katy Gaulip, Elizabeth Mamros, Josh Elders, Raashmi Krishnasamy, Karen and Jeff Spindler, Mikasa McKnight, Egan Paul, Livi Redden, Daniel Krajovic, Sonya Ring, Leah Steirer, Carrie Buchanan, Trevor and Christine McCure, Molly McAfee, Alex Shackleton, Bailey Dennis, Nick Wojack, Carly Newberg, Sean Harrison, Ian Sopko, Amy Wang, Christina Iafelice, Lea Breckner, Melanie Fang, Frank Provo, Marcia and Dick McCracken, Jennifer Rompilla, Mary Ann Hanicak, Freddy Smith, Mary Jeanne Nobers, and Char Dillart.

AUTHOR'S NOTE

All the people and stories in this book are real; however, I have used pseudonyms for several interviewees to protect their privacy.

APPENDIX

INTRODUCTION

Kim Swims. "Story: At the Podium." Accessed October 2, 2020. https://kimswims.com/journey-1.

Stories. "How Kim Chambers Conquered the 7 Deadliest Swims." May 28, 2015. Video, 4:47. https://www.youtube.com/watch?v=tob6tCYC8DE.

Youn, Soo Jeong, and Raquel Halfond. "How to Cope with Traumatic Stress." *American Psychological Association.* October 30, 2019. https://www.apa.org/topics/traumatic-stress.

CHAPTER 1

John Hopkins Medicine. "Olfactory Neuroblastoma." Accessed March 2, 2020. https://www.hopkinsmedicine.org/health/conditions-and-diseases/olfactory-neuroblastoma.

UPMC: Life Changing Medicine. "Olfactory Neuroblastoma (Esthesioneuroblastoma)." Accessed February 28, 2020. https://www.upmc.com/services/neurosurgery/brain/conditions/brain-tumors/olfactory-neuroblastoma.

CHAPTER 3

DeArdo, Bryan. "Ryan Shazier Celebrates His Continued Recovery on Two-Year Anniversary of Spinal Injury." *CBS Sports,* December 6, 2019. https://www.cbssports.com/nfl/news/ryan-shazier-celebrates-his-continued-recovery-on-two-year-anniversary-of-spinal-injury/.

Giffords, Gabby, and Mark Kelly. "The New Year Is a Time for Hope, Even after Tragedy." *Time,* November 30, 2017. https://time.com/5041049/gabby-giffords-husband-after-shooting/.

Hawking, Stephen. "Biography." Accessed on March 16, 2020. https://www.hawking.org.uk/contact.

Kaminer, Debra, and Gillian Eagle. "Trauma as a Crisis of Meaning" In *Traumatic Stress in South Africa*, 60–79. Johannesburg, South Africa: Wits University Press, 2010.

Mental Health Foundation. "The Impact of Traumatic Events on Mental Health." Accessed on March 2, 2020. https://www.mentalhealth.org.uk/publications/impact-traumatic-events-mental-health.

Meyers, Laurie. "Grief: Going Beyond Death and Stages." *Counseling Today, A Publication of the American*

Counseling Association, October 27, 2016. https://ct.counseling.org/2016/10/grief-going-beyond-death-stages/.

Moore, Catherine. "What Is the Negativity Bias and How Can It Be Overcome?" *Positive Psychology,* March 8, 2020. https://positivepsychology.com/3-steps-negativity-bias/.

Rowell, Kevin, and Rebecca Thomley. "Recovering Emotionally from Disaster." *American Psychological Association,* 2013. https://www.apa.org/topics/recovering-disasters.

Substance Abuse and Mental Health Services Administration (SAMHSA). "Chapter 3 Understanding the Impact of Trauma." *Trauma-Informed Care in Behavioral Health Services.* 2014. https://www.ncbi.nlm.nih.gov/books/NBK207191/.

CHAPTER 4

Hawking, Stephen. *My Brief History.* United Kingdom: Bantam Books, 2013.

McCleary, Kathleen. "Life Is Good: The Story of Mark Kelly and Gabby Giffords." *Parade,* February 10, 2017. https://parade.com/545964/kmccleary/life-is-good-the-story-of-mark-kelly-and-gabby-giffords/.

NFL. "Pittsburgh Steelers Linebacker Ryan Shazier Talks about His Relentless Recovery." 2019. Video, 6:28. https://www.nfl.com/videos/pittsburgh-steelers-linebacker-ryan-shazier-talks-about-his-relentless-re-403199.

Shazier, Ryan (@shazier). "Thank You ....." Instagram video, September 9, 2020. https://www.instagram.com/p/CE6zFGXJl8m/.

TED. "Gabby Giffords and Mark Kelly: Be Passionate. Be Courageous. Be Your Best." April 11, 2014. Video, 18:48. https://www.youtube.com/watch?v=M6TMSQWI9m4.

Todor, Rob. "Ryan Shazier to Present Inspirational Story of Recovery at Record-Courier's Best of Preps Event." *Record-Courier,* June 6, 2019. https://www.record-courier.com/news/20190606/ryan-shazier-to-present-inspirational-story-of-recovery-at-record-couriers-best-of-preps-event.

CHAPTER 5

Eva, Amy L. "Four Ways to Gain Perspective on Negative Events." *Greater Good Magazine,* September 12, 2017. https://greatergood.berkeley.edu/article/item/four_ways_to_gain_perspective_on_negative_events.

Marsh, James, dir. *The Theory of Everything.* London, England: Working Title Films, 2014. DVD.

CHAPTER 6

TEDx. "Brené Brown: The Power of Vulnerability." June 1, 2010. Video, 20:19. https://www.ted.com/talks/brene_brown_the_power_of_vulnerability?language=en.

CHAPTER 7

Lougheed, Oleg. "Life Won't Give You Anything You Can't Handle | Joel de Carteret." July 23, 2018. In *Overcoming Odds Podcast*. Podcast. MP3 audio, 49:21. https://podcasts.apple.com/us/podcast/the-overcoming-odds-podcast/id1292465138?i=1000416459993.

Resilience Research Centre. "About Us." Accessed August 23, 2020. https://resilienceresearch.org/about-resilience/.

CHAPTER 8

Feldman, Christina, and Willem Kuyken. "Compassion in the Landscape of Suffering." *Contemporary Buddhism - An Interdisciplinary Journal* 1, no. 12 (2011): 143–155.

Uhrig, Jim. *Partners 4 Life: The Importance of Partners in Surviving an Organ Transplant.* Bloomington: iUniverse, 2014.

CHAPTER 9

Frankl, Viktor E. *Man's Search for Meaning.* Boston: Beacon Press, 2006.

Robert Half. "Adaptability Skills." Accessed August 24, 2020. https://www.roberthalf.co.nz/career-advice/career-development/adaptability-skills.

CHAPTER 10

Greater Good Science Center. "Robert Emmons: Benefits of Gratitude." November 19, 2010. Video, 10:35. https://www.youtube.com/watch?v=RRrnfGf5aWE&feature=emb_logo.

TED. "Stacey Kramer: The Best Gift I Ever Survived." October 8, 2010. Video, 6:26. https://www.youtube.com/watch?v=PKbet4RdSo4.

CHAPTER 11

Craig, Lydia. "Are You Suffering from Imposter Syndrome? Ways to Identify and Deal with Feelings of Self-Doubt in Grad School." *American Psychological Association,* September 2018. https://www.apa.org/science/about/psa/2018/09/imposter-syndrome.

TED. "'To This Day' . . . for the Bullied and Beautiful | Shane Koyczan." March 8, 2013. Video, 12:03. https://www.youtube.com/watch?v=sa1iS1MqUy4.

CHAPTER 12

Eleanor Brownn. "Most Popular Quotes by Eleanor Brownn." Accessed August 26, 2020. http://www.eleanorbrownn.com/.

Lieberman, Charlotte. "How Self-Care Becomes So Much Work." *Harvard Business Review,* August 10, 2018. https://hbr.org/2018/08/how-self-care-became-so-much-work.

CHAPTER 15

Anxiety and Depression Association of America. "Highlights: Workplace Stress & Anxiety Disorders Survey." Accessed on February 12, 2020. https://adaa.org/workplace-stress-anxiety-disorders-survey.

Naber, Andrew. "One Third of Your Life Is Spent at Work." *Gettysburg College News,* May 16, 2020. https://www.gettysburg.edu/news/stories?id=79db7b34-630c-4f49-ad32-4ab9ea48e72b.

Smith, Melinda, Jeanne Segal, and Lawrence Robinson. "Burnout Prevention and Treatment." HelpGuide, October 2019. https://www.helpguide.org/articles/stress/burnout-prevention-and-recovery.htm.

Steveson, Mason. "Employee Burnout Statistics You Need to Know." HR Exchange Network, January 16, 2020. https://www.hrexchangenetwork.com/employee-engagement/news/employee-burnout-statistics-you-need-to-know.

The American Institute of Stress. "42 Worrying Workplace Stress Statistics." September 25, 2019. https://www.stress.org/42-worrying-workplace-stress-statistics.

CPSIA information can be obtained
at www.ICGtesting.com
Printed in the USA
BVHW041456211220
596048BV00006B/11